Historical Study Of

AGRARIAN RELATIONS IN NEPAL

(1846-1951)

Historical Study Of

AGRARIAN RELATIONS IN NEPAL

(1846-1951)

by

Shanker Thapa
MA, B.L., Ph.D.
Associate Professor

ADROIT PUBLISHERS
DELHI-110 053

Published by
ADROIT PUBLISHERS
C-8/2, Yamuna Vihar, Delhi-110 053
e-mail: akhilbooks@yahoo.com
Phone: 3266030

ISBN : 81-87392-17-7

Layout by
Sudhir Kumar Vatsa

Laser Typeset by
Nidhi Laser Point, Shahdara, Delhi.
e-mail: nidhi_vatsa@hotmail.com
Phone : 2825424

Printed in India by
B.K. Offset, Shahdara Delhi-110 032

To

My Mother

FOREWORD

The book entitled **'Historical Study of Agrarian Relations in Nepal** : 1846-1951' is a scholarly research work of my student-cum-colleague Associate Professor Dr. Shanker Thapa, one of the promising rising historians of Nepal.

Dr. Shanker Thapa is a very hard working research scholar who has taken much pains in completing this book. So, far I know he has consulted most of the authentic documents available for a researcher in Nepal. His dedication and hard labour are much appreciable. I must say that a research work is never ending task. As much I hope this work will prompt other scholars also to contribute more on the subject in different aspects.

The present work 'Historical Study of Agrarian Relations in Nepal 1846-1951' is the first one of this kind. Agro-economy is the main aspect of the Nepalese economy. Cultivation of land is almost the only source of income in the remote parts of the country. In this profession, females played/play major role which is not duly acknowledged by the male dominant society.

In a country like Nepal covered by huge mountains where cultivation is the most important rather the only occupation of the common mass, a study on the relations between state and landlords, landlords and tenants, state and tillers of land is most pertinent one. Such studies will open the eyes of the decision makers so that the country and country men can reap the harvest of the right decisions. This work, I feel , is such a historical research work, which can serve as the eye opener to all concerned people of Nepal. I hope and wish him to continue the research work on related themes, so that further details of the subject will come out. This is not an end, it is the beginning. Once again I would like to congratulate Dr. Thapa for his scholarly work.

Prof. Dr. T.R.Vaidya

PREFACE

The term agrarian relations refers to rural production relations and inter relationships in agrarian society. The evaluation of the traditional structure of an agrarian society, tenurial conditions, production and distribution processes, role of the agrarian groups in the process , rural economic interactions, and so on, are basic components which are essential for understanding agrarian relations in a particular society. Thus, the land use patterns, production process, distribution of products, rural financial behaviour, and rent-credit systems have a profound impact on the nature of agrarian relations .The agrarian system in Nepal from 1846 -1964 was traditional and conservative. The feudal elements which were prevalent in agriculture during that period still exist to some extent in rural societies in spite of repeated attempts to reform traditional agriculture, and persisted even after promulgation of the Land Reforms Act of 1964. The traditional agricultural system remained almost unchanged throughout the century of the Ranas' rule in Nepal, but the end of the regime was followed by gradual changes in the traditional agrarian structure.

The conceptual paradigm of 'agrarian relations' has various components but the context in which it is used in this book denotes the basic relations between different hierarchies in the agrarian structure, analyzing their rights, duties, and privileges as well as, their respective roles in the production process. However, the existing systems of agrarian relations favored the land owning elite at the expense of the toiling peasantry.

The peasants cultivated land without any significant rights, and the entire means of production was controlled by the privileged classes. Therefore, In Nepal, land was the property of those who did not cultivate it. The separation of land ownership from cultivation continued to bear important theme in agrarian relations. The peasant cultivators cultivated land either as sharecroppers or tenant farmers and retained insignificant amount of grains after paying rent and taxes to the land owners or intermediaries. From the very beginning, the peasant economy was vulnerable, and the cultivators were also required to satisfy the needs of the privileged classes, who tended to exact as much rent from them as possible. However, they did not play any kind of role in the production process. This was the basic situation that prevailed in agriculture during the Ranas' regime.

In my entire academic life, Prof. Dr. Choung Hae Chang of the Academy of Korean Studies, Seongnam-si, Korea has greater contribution. What I am academically now is only because of his constant guidance and tireless effort. Therefore, his efforts brought me at this level of academic pursuit. So, I must express sincere gratitude and best regards to him.

While writing this book, many prominent Nepali historians provided me with valuable help and advice. It would not have been possible to write this book without their help. I am very much indebted to all of my professors and other scholars of prominence for their help and creative support. I must express my sincere gratitude to Prof. Dr. Tulasi Ram Vaidya, Professor and Head of Central Department of History, Tribhuvan University, Kathmandu whose invaluable supervision enabled me to prepare this volume. Any faults that may be found in this book are mine. I am indebted to him for his support, comments on the manuscript and proper guidance in the use of materials. I am also very grateful to him for having written the foreword.

I would also like to express sincere gratitude to Professors Dr. Prem Raman Uprety and Dr. Kedar Nath Banstola, for their help.

I must express my sincere gratitude to Dr. Vijaya K.

Manandhar, Associate Professor and Mr. Bhaveswor Pangeni, Lecturer of the Central Department of History for their help in reading the manuscript and giving valuable suggestions.

Thanks are also due to Bishnu Raj Ojha of T.U. Central Library, Nva Raj Karki (National Library, Patan), and Bishwa Nath Dhungel (Keshar Library, Kathmandu), staff members of the Record section of the Department of Revenue H.M.G. for their support during material collection.

I must make a special mention of the Thapas, Nirmala, Sizan and Susan, and express heartily thanks to them for their good will and help.

Millicent A. Pugh from Illinois, USA deserves a special share of thanks for doing a painstaking job of editing the entire manuscript and giving valuable suggestions to make it worthy of reading. She did an excellent job of correcting my style of linguistic expression in English, and I heartily appreciate her help .

At last but not least, I would also like to express thanks to Mr. Krishna Kumar Thapa who did all of the computer related work that was required in order to prepare this book.

Dr. Shanker Thapa
Associate Professor
Central Department of History
Tribhuvan University
Kathmandu, Nepal
Tel: + 977-1-611470

CONTENTS

	Foreword	*vii*
	Preface	*ix*
1.	Framework of The Study	1
2.	Agrarian Structure of The Nepalese Society	15
3.	Agrarian Production Relations	54
4.	Status of The Cultivators	89
5.	The Changing Pattern of Relations	123
6.	Conclusion	160
	Bibliography	176
	Glossary	187
	Appendices	193
	Index	198

CHAPTER I

FRAMEWORK OF THE STUDY

Research Problem and Theme

The study of land and agriculture and other related variables particularly the relationships has significant importance in understanding the economic activities of a traditional society. In such a society, land is given top priority because it is one of the principal source of income and a sign of prestige and dignity and at the same time, is a secure form of property. Since long ago, land has been an important type of property in Nepalese society . So, the overall scenario will be depicted here so as to define the research problem that will be dealt in other chapters.

Although economy has remained subordinate to politics throughout history,the economic aspect of a nation has played a vital role in determining national politics and the political behaviour of the people. In the past, politics was always affected by the economy although the latter was entirely based on traditional agrarian activities. Until now, ordinary people have not been given due credit in recorded history. However, the role of the ordinary populace in shaping the history of a country can not be easily ignored. The cultivators of the country are responsible for the agricultural production process. The history of agriculture is important in order to understand the entire historical background and establishes a link between history and economy. Therefore, the study of a given society in this paradigm has great importance in tracing the historical significance of traditional types of agrarian relations. It is considered to be even more significant in the heterogeneous society of Nepal, where one caste group remained dominant over other cultivating communities. In fact, there was no specific agrarian caste, but all castes were involved in agriculture in one way or another. Usually, the high caste groups remained dominant over the peasantry. In general, the *Brahmins* and the *Chhetriyas* remained more dominant in agrarian relations by controlling considerable areas of land as landlords of different categories. The cultivators in general belonged to all caste groups and ethnicities. The Nepalese gentry had a tight grip on entire farming communities by controlling entire means of production, agricultural and otherwise. The primary interests of various groups in land was necessarily limited to obtaining a share in agrarian produce and thereby enjoying other relative privileges created by their respective status in the hierarchy of agrarian relations. In Nepal, history bears witness to the fact that land was given higher importance by all sections of the society because it is the principal means of production or capital formation. It was also the major form of property. Therefore, possession of land with property rights was always the symbol of a higher social status. In fact, in the pre-industrial traditional societies, the absence of other sources of income and the lack of a means of production other than the land led to a higher concentration of population on agricultural land. This is the reason why land is considered to be a matter of prestige, dignity and higher social status to its owner, which ensured their fixed income status. At the same time, it also guaranteed their higher status in the agrarian hierarchy.

During the Rana regime, all the land, both cultivated and cultivable was divided into different types and sub-types. Basically, it was divided into *Raikar* and the *Kipat*. The other subtypes i.e. the *Birta, Jagir, Guthi, Rakam, Jimidari* etc. originated because the state gave absolute land ownership rights to individuals. This process of transfer of land rights has contributed to the development of a special kind of agrarian relations. In all these tenures, the landowning elite both the resident and absentee landlords had the upper hand and enjoyed both ownership and property rights on the land. The relations between cultivators and the landowning aristocracy remained almost unchanged throughout the Rana regime and, to some extent, after the end of the regime also. It is obvious that the rights of the involved parties, which include the landowners, landholding intermediaries, and actual cultivators, differed from each other according to the nature of the tenure. The *Birta* owners, *Rajautas, Jagirdars*, royal families, nobility and other individuals of higher socio-political status held large areas of land and estates mainly in the Tarai as *Birta*. The importance of the Tarai has grown since 1860s, when the British rulers in India expanded a railroad along the Nepal border. It further increased the number of landlords, mainly the absentees in the Tarai, because many influential families obtained *Birtas* in these areas, and this situation virtually made the entire Tarai a kind of undeclared colony within Nepal.

The absentees appointed intermediaries and rented land to cultivators through them. The intermediaries grew to be one of most powerful elite classes in the hierarchy of agrarian relations, along with their masters, and remained so for centuries. Both of them presented unwanted financial burdens for the peasants. The practice of absenteeism was never desirable or favourable for productive agriculture because of the burden created by it. The land ownership in Nepal before 1964 was unequally distributed. Ownership and cultivation are two important aspects of agricultural development, but in Nepal, ownership and cultivation were separated during the Rana regime and thereafter. The separation of the two, i.e. the rights of ownership and the practice of cultivation, had been one of the most widespread practices in Nepal.

The big landlords rented their land for cultivation to the poor cultivators, who had no other means of production under their control in order to survive and, at the same time, compelled them to offer higher bids for rent to obtain land for cultivation. These kinds of transactions were made through the local intermediaries. The involvement of the latter also created an extra financial burden for the peasants. The practice further strengthened the separation of ownership and cultivation. In fact, the unity of ownership and cultivation has been an important aspect in agricultural growth, and brings about significant changes in the production. In fact, it increases production because such unity is in itself an incentive to peasants, but the then prevailing situation was such that unity between the two was almost impossible. The privileged classes in the agrarian society obtained ownership of vast areas of land, which were not possible for them to cultivate by themselves. The entire rural mass belonged to a cultivating class deprived of land. The Rana policy during the century long regime was never favourable for the cultivating peasants.

In general, the peasant community remained in deplorable conditions. The conditions of the *Jagir* and *Birta* cultivators were the most vulnerable and the worst of all. The owners used every unjust means to collect rent and levies if the latter failed to pay even due to crop failure, etc. The *Jagirdars*, on the other hand, in certain cases were entitled to collect rent in advance, for which cultivators were compelled to borrow money at excessively higher rates of rent. Similarly, the *Jagirdars* and *Birta* owners were empowered to use force and detain their cultivators if they failed to pay. The latter also had to pay excessively high rates of rent and could be evicted at the will of the owners. The *Jagirdars* and the Birta owners exercised absolute land rights. The peasants paid more than 2/3 of gross produce as rent, excluding other customary levies. Even in the Jimidari tenure in Jhapa district, the cultivators cultivated land under most unfavourable conditions, and sometimes they paid all of their grain to the *Jimidars* for rent, taxes and interest on borrowings and could retain only straw as their share.[1] This was the overall condition of the peasantry before 1951. The legal enactment during 1950s started to introduce reforms in the existing system. In fact, the intended reforms were the result

1. Louis J. Wallinsky, *Selected Papers of Wolf Ladejinsky : Agrarian Feforms asan Unfunished Business,* New Your : Oxford University Press, 1977, pp. 307-315.

of pressure created by the peasant organizations in the country.

The landlords and other privileged groups remained dominant in the agrarian hierarchy. The most significant aspect of this situation for them was that they were able to control the entire rural population. It further contributed to the Rana regime by providing smooth running for the administration. The Rana regime was mainly concerned with the maintenance of law and order and the collection of land revenue. Therefore, the rulers never attempted to improve the condition of the peasantry. The ruling elite favoured the land owning class. Most of the big landlords were royalty, the Ranas, their relatives, supporters, and nobility. Thus, the structure of the society, the importance of land as a means of production, land holding as a sign of dignity and social prestige, the involvement of intermediaries in land, agrarian activities and the pattern of agrarian relations all played vital roles in the agrarian relations in Nepal. All of these historical realities involved three basic issues - relations between owners and cultivators, the state and the tenants and; intermediaries, peasant cultivators, and sharecroppers. In fact, these types of relationships obviously represented the relations between landowning and other privileged communities and tenants or cultivators of any kind. These basic relationships created various kinds of rights and duties, which later played vital role in the continuity of such relationships. The higher strata in the agrarian hierarchy enjoyed various land rights, whereas it was the duty of a cultivator to pay big amount of rent and customary levies. The regular payment of rent and taxes were the only way to continue the maintenance of cultivation rights. On the other hand, rent and taxes also played a significant role in determining the nature of relations between the agrarian groups. If private property is abandoned, then all unnatural divisions in the society disappear. The differences between privileged and non-privileged also disappears.[2] Marxist literature explains that the entire history of mankind

2. Meszaros, Ist Van, *Marx's Theory of Alienation,* London : Merlin Press, 1986, p. 77.

consists of nothing but the betterment of man through human labour. Productive activity is, therefore, the mediator in the subject object relationship.[3] Thus, tenancy, rent and taxes, etc. were driving forces in agrarian relations.

During the Rana regime, both sharecropping and fixed rate tenancies were in practice. These were widely accepted systems of rent collection. It is very much important to note that, in Nepal, the state was the biggest landlord. It was the ultimate proprietor of all land. But it gave its right to collect rent to individuals on certain occasions. Therefore, although the state was the biggest landlord, its share in agrarian produce was only 13.5% on the 'A' grade Raikar land, whereas the individual landowners and cultivators retained the remaining 86.5% of total yield. The share of cultivators on tax exempt *Birta* and *Jagir* land was almost 32% of the total production, which excludes customary levies and *Koshelees*. The state had no direct relations with the actual cultivator and they were not even registered in revenue records. The owners were registered as tax payers in such records. Therefore, the cultivators as a class were hardly important for the state, because it was the landowner, not the cultivators, who paid taxes on land irrespective of cultivation. The direct relationship between the state and landowners, and later, with the intermediaries of various types, virtually ignored this class. The revenue records maintained by the government contained only the names of tax paying landowners as tenants, and not those of the actual cultivators. So, the state hardly benefited from the system at that time in terms of financial gain. The right of rent collection was given to individual owners. It was the land owner who was the actual beneficiary, but they had no financial or material obligation as prescribed by the law to improve agriculture or increase production. The system, although it seemed economically worse, helped in the maintenance of political stability because the upper class had a grip on the entire

3. T.B. Bottomore, *Introduction to Kari Marx's Early Writings*, London : 1963, pp. 44-45.

population. This type of traditional relationship continued to exist throughout the century, even after the political changes of 1951. But in due course of time, various *Rukkas* (Royal verdicts), *Sawals* (Regulations), *Ains* (laws) etc. were enacted and issued, which attempted to define such relationship. But with the exception of insignificant and minor changes, such legal enactments could not bring about radical changes, and were of no historical or socio-economic value. In fact, any change in the existing traditional agrarian system was obviously meant to minimize the rights and privileges of the land owning elite, but the situation was such that it was almost impossible to make decisions against the interests of the land owning aristocracy. The large scale owners (absentees), *Jagirdars* and Birtawalas were mainly the Ranas, Shahs and nobility. Therefore, the Rana premiers were reluctant to move against them or harm their interests; they were even compelled not to do so. The existing system presupposes an already fixed, political relationship between production and appropriation. If the surplus product was not distributed on an equitable basis, the following situation arises in the normal functioning of the society. The smaller the amount of surplus product, the more exclusive the appropriating class must be if the purpose of accumulation is to be reached. If conflict is to be avoided, one must find a regulative principle or institution capable of establishing continuity.

This kind of system had various drawbacks in terms of agrarian economic development and the welfare of tenants. It was the peasantry who had to bear all financial and material burdens of the landowning elite. The actual cultivators were responsible for completing all of the necessary stages of cultivation and production i.e. ploughing, fertilizing, supplying seeds, irrigation, etc. But on the other hand, the owners had no obligation of any kind, although they exacted almost 2/3 of the gross produce as rent. The peasants lived in bare subsistence and at the mercy of the landowners and the intermediaries. The *Jagir* and *Birta* cultivators lived vulnerable life. Almost 2/3 of the gross produce was paid as rent which was necessary to retain cultivation rights.

However, tenancy rights were not secured until 1964. Therefore, they were evicted or appointed at the will of the owners or the intermediaries. In this way, cultivation itself was less important than obtaining ownership of land.

There was no incentive given to peasants to increase production at that time. It was a general practice to bid for land for cultivation. The higher bidder was usually given cultivation rights, evicting the old tenant without considering social relations. The only concern was to increase the amount of rent and taxes. In this situation, rural landlessness and unemployment compelled them to agree to all conditions to continue cultivation. Once they agreed to the stipulated amount of rent, they were normally permitted to remain on the land. This was a customary practice but it was not necessary for the landowners to follow it, because even if the regime ordered them not to evict the old tenants if they agreed to the stipulated rent, the owners sometimes evicted them without considering the old rules. Normally, the poor cultivators did not protest against such arbitrary eviction, but no doubt the ruler would have taken necessary action if it was reported.

The existing land ownership has kept owners and cultivators in bilateral relations founded on the principle of duties rather than rights. It is very important to note that land was the property of those who did not till it. Thus, ownership and cultivation were separate. This has been the most significant aspect of Nepal's land holding system - land was not the property of the cultivators. They were concerned only with initiating cultivation and paying a share of produce as rent and taxes and fulfilling other material needs of the owners. They could hold cultivation rights through the regular payment of rents and taxes, but tenancy was insecure and not protected. As a result, the lives of the cultivators depended on the mercy of the landowning classes. The rights or status and financial conditions of the peasant community varied to some extent on the basis of tenure they cultivated, but in general, their economic condition was unsatisfactory. The cultivators in *Raikar, Birta, Guthi* and *Jagir* tenures differed from one another.

The relationship among different agrarian groups was fundamentally based on economic terms which ignored all other components, including the social factor. The peasant economy, lack of monetization in the nineteenth century in rural Nepal, and the lack of adequate means of production led to increasing poverty among the peasantry. Consequently, the increasing rural indebtedness remained forever, and peasants lacked credit to perform various kinds of work both in productive and non-productive sectors, such as initiating production activities, celebrating festivals, payment of rent (mainly in *Jagir*)[4] and performing rituals. For all these activities, the peasants were compelled to ask for credit from the village moneylenders, who were usually the local resident landowners. But the need for credit had a multiple and relative impact on the peasants' economy and social lives as well. The impact was always negative. The nature of credit was such that once it was contracted, it was almost impossible to extricate one's self from the debt chain. The excessively higher rates of interest and other associated obligations of a debtor destroyed the entire individual peasant economy.

This kind of deteriorated agrarian economy, burden presented by the privileged classes in the structural hierarchy, lack of adequate means of production, high pressure of the population on the land, the dominance of the Nepalese gentry over the cultivating community, the role of village moneylenders, and the level of exploitation led to the creation of widespread discontent and dissatisfaction among the Nepalese peasantry. Such discontent has been accumulating since long ago. Until 1951, the level of dissatisfaction rose to the point at which an outlet was required. Along with the anti-Rana movement, the establishment of Nepal's Communist Party was an attempt to provide relief to the dissatisfied peasant groups and encourage them to revolt against the usurers. Most

4. Sometimes, the *Jagirdars* were also authorized to collect rent in advance for multiple years from the peasants who generally could not pay as demanded by the landowners.

of the peasant movements were ideologically communist oriented. Their activities and agitation were intended to bring about changes in the traditional structure of the society and the economic exploitation of the peasantry. The peasant movements organized in both the Tarai and the hills were violent in nature. In fact, they were intended to bring about radical changes in the rural economy and reform the traditional type of agrarian relations. During the 1950s, almost all the peasant movements were led by the Communist activists. The democratic leaders under the banner of the Nepali Congress (N.C.) also attempted to satisfy the toiling peasantry by introducing agricultural policies aimed at introducing changes in the traditional type of agriculture. Several acts were passed under Nepali Congress rule and eradicated certain unfavourable elements from the land. But it should be noted that the Nepali Congress itself was comprised of several big landlords. The most popular demand of the peasants during the period was- "*Land to the tiller*", which attracted peasants. Besides, the activists did not fail to include economic, socio-political and material demands as well. Therefore, these kinds of activities which emerged at the end of the Rana regime finally contributed to bring about changes in the existing pattern of agrarian relations. In later decades, the promulgation of different laws changed the basic nature of such relationships and affected the rural economy. As the result of peasant unity, they were given various rights, rent was fixed at one half of gross produce, traditional tenures were abolished and tenancy was also protected by enacting the Land Reforms Act of 1964.

It was the duty of a cultivator to keep the owners fully satisfied by paying compulsory rent, exorbitant taxes, and providing various other services. In fact, the rent and tax composition and its payment shaped the nature of existing agrarian relations in all types of tenures. The relationship between such groups was fundamentally based on economic terms which ignored all other factors or ties.

The peasant community did not enjoy permanent occupancy rights, nor did they enjoy protected tenurial rights. This arrangement witnessed marginal changes in the latter period of the regime, which duly affected existing agrarian relations. The practice of absenteeism and other types of landlordism, intermediaries, rent composition and customs and statutes all resulted in hardships for the peasant community. The superstructure of agrarian relations as such, served the immediate needs of the government and the landed aristocracy. The relations throughout the century were characterized by age old oppression and exploitation of the peasantry. It kept agricultural production stagnant and progress non-existent. The rapacious landowners and intermediaries were legally permitted to act without restrictions and continued appropriation of the surpluses.

This historical tradition influenced land holding practices even after 1951. Even at present, some of the features of land holding prevalent during the Rana regime continue to exist in many parts of the country, but the legal enactment or promulgation of different acts attempted to introduce changes in the existing form of agrarian relations. The basic nature of relations is different now. Some of the hierarchies in the agrarian social structure have been abolished by law. Such changes in the situation are favourable for peasants, and led to gradual evolution of peasants' rights on the land. The legacy of ruthless exploitation of the Nepalese peasantry and the carelessness of the rulers in making any changes in the traditional types of agrarian structure and conventional production systems thereby protecting the interests of the landowning elite led to increased demands for land reforms. So, the interests of owners and cultivators collided at this point. Such a clash was more costly to the peasants because many of the protests against the system that prevailed during the Rana regime ended in the suppression of many peasant protests right after 1951. Most of the landowners were in favour of crushing peasant rebellions and rejected any kind of reforms or introduction of changes in the existing system. Thus, most of the Tarai districts such as Bara, Parsa, Rautahat, Sarlahi, Dhanusha, Mahottari, Siraha, Saptari, Banke, Bardia, Rupandehi and Dang including some of the hill districts (Palpa etc.) witnessed peasant movements against the usurers, landowners, intermediaries and local revenue officials. The peasants continued to act against those who went against their interests. This was an attempt to improve the peasant economy thereby bringing about changes in the peasants' status and in the existing form of agrarian relations. The agrarian structure and agrarian relations during the Rana regime were a continuation of the system that prevailed before the emergence of the Rana regime. The relations, powers and privileges of landowners, both residents and absentees, the conditions of rural indebtedness and credit composition, the attitude of village moneylenders, and the inextricable chain of debt were factors that prompted the demand for speedy changes in the agrarian system. The peasantry remained as the force of production for centuries without obtaining any significant land rights. It is painful to know that the land was not the property of those who were tied to it as its production force for many generations. On the contrary, it was the property of the owners who were entrusted with the rights of ownership. The peasantry remained unsatisfied with the existing situation, so, they were organized under the leadership of various organizations and activists to fight against the enemies of their class. They struggled and fought against the usurers and demanded that land should belong to those who till it. They further demanded the correction of kinds of exploitation. The formation of peasant forces brought them face to face with the situation and class conflict rose to its height. The peasants' unity created a force which could not be easily ignored by the rulers. Their pressure ultimately brought about changes in the nature of agrarian relations. As a result, various reforms were introduced to improve the situation in later years.

This book examines the agrarian relations and changes in the basic nature of such relationships focusing on the agrarian social structure and land control, the production process, the channelization of production and changes in the role and status of the agrarian classes. In this analysis, the economic factor remains vital to all other social factors. The rural economic structure basically debt composition and the financial burden on the cultivating community is considered to be very significant in the analysis. The use, control and ownership of land is also vital in the analysis of the practical aspect of Nepalese agriculture in the given period.

In the 1950s, the Nepalese peasantry was gradually liberated from the old tight grip of the Rana aristocracy and their associates. The increasing level of discontent among the peasantry against glaring acts of oppression and coercion by the landlords, which was influenced by left wing ideology, played a significant role in bringing about changes in agrarian structure as well as in existing agrarian relations. The decade itself established the peasant community as a force that could bring about changes in the political economy of agriculture. This ability of the oppressed peasantry can be analysed within the paradigm of left wing politics. The peasant leadership, politics, interests and affiliation with the Communists in the broader perspective have enduring consequences in the future development and evolution of the peasant society and course of national politics. These frames of reference and the issues mentioned above provide a framework for the analysis of the structure of Nepalese society in terms of agriculture and agrarian relations at the practical level.

Concepts

The agrarian structure is comprised of various classes, roughly classified as privileged and non- privileged classes. The concept of class has been used in a Marxian sense to imply objective economic conditions or unity of communal economic interests. It is the relationship among classes of persons involved in agriculture and landed interests and social groups that occupy certain positions in the society in relation to land control and its use.

Various other concepts, such as agrarian relations, peasants' rights, movements etc. are also used in this book. Under the general scheme of this book, agrarian relations tends to denote a general relationship between all involved parties in agriculture in general and landlords and tenants in particular. It is necessarily an economic relationship and the parties' interests involved in particular piece of land. The sharing of rights, and claim to the produce of the soil is the core of the relationship.

The term 'peasant' is exclusively used to denote the cultivating community with or without rights. It denotes to the community of peasants as a whole. Basically, it is divided on the basis of Lenin's division of peasants. A large majority of Nepali peasants consists of middle and poor peasants.

Similarly, 'peasant movement' used as a blanket term in the book means a factor that introduces changes in agrarian relations as well as forces reshaping of the involved parties' interests. Thus, it refers to the attempts of peasants to change the prevailing system for a better future or to seek redress for particular grievances without intending to overthrow the system. The term 'right' is used broadly to indicate land rights such as the rights of the land owners, the tenancy rights and the right to cultivate.

Besides, these terms, several other terminology are also used to analyse agrarian relations and other related situations.

Scope of the study

Although the title of the research seems to be general or vague, it deals with the relationship between landowners and cultivators. The specific relationship between privileged and non-privileged groups in agriculture is dealt with mainly on the basis of the status of agrarian groups.

This research is chronologically limited to the period from 1846 to 1964. It places special emphasis on the second half of the period; but it does not ignore the first half of the regime, also taking it into account. In the same way, some relevant references are drawn from different activities which began after 1964. The agrarian system of a nation has various independent themes to investigate through research, but this research is confined to the analysis of agrarian social structure and agrarian relations which determine the relations between different levels in the Nepalese agrarian system in the given period.

* * *

CHAPTER II

AGRARIAN STRUCTURE OF THE NEPALESE SOCIETY

Introduction:

The analysis of the structural pattern of an agrarian society is a key component for understanding the basic nature of agrarian and production relationships between the landlords and tenants, intermediaries and actual cultivators, landowners and land holding intermediaries and so on. It represents the agrarian society, ways of mutual interaction and understanding, whereas land, as the major component, is related to its use, control and pattern of ownership.

The state itself remains very powerful in all kinds of land related matters. The land rights of individuals came to exist only because the state transferred its right and privileges to individuals. The state has been the main and biggest owner of land, having full control over land both in India and Nepal.[1] The classical Hindu religious texts mention land, its cultivation and use in an appropriate way. Mann in his famous treatise *Manusmriti* has also mentioned land. He expressed views on agriculture and land ownership in a systematic way.[2] The state had the right to grant land or exact a share of its gross product.

---

1. Shirin Akhtar, *The Role of Zamindars in Bengal,* Dhaka : Asiatic Society of Bangladesh, 1982, pp. 3-5.
2. B.H. Baden-Powel, *The Indian Village Community,* Delhi : Cosmo Publications, 1972, pp. 188-204.

In India, even the Mughal Empire feudalized the agrarian system. In an agrarian society, the peasants work to satisfy the interests of their masters.

The lack of other sources of income, a low per capita amount of land as the fixed form of property, the rights of a landowner, etc. gave top importance to land ownership. It represented a status symbol of economic or political security.[3] Nepalese society, whose economy was based on and heavily dependent on agriculture, gave top priority to the acquisition of land as property. Therefore, it occupied the highest value in contemporary Nepalese society. It has been considered to be a secured form of property. The possession of land not only provides economic subsistence, but also confers social status and dignity. For this reason, the landowners were prestigious and influential in the society, and wealth, privilege and prestige are still associated with ownership. The landlords and other privileged classes not only had higher incomes but also enjoyed various privileges and rights in terms of land and people. It helped them control the landless population in different ways.[4] The favourites of the ruling class were granted land as rewards either subject to nominal tax or tax free, because the state designated the right of land ownership to its favourites and supporters. The ruling elite also became the owners of large areas of land.[5] The ownership of land has several benefits. It provided the right to control a certain area of land and the inhabitants residing in the area.[6] The state gave its land rights

---

3. Dietmar Rothermund, '*Government, Landlord and Tenant In India 1875-1900*' (reprinted from : The Economic & Social Hisotyr Journal- vol. VI, No.-4, Dec. 1969), Heidelberg : Sourth asia Insitute of the University of Heidelberg, 1969, p. 351.
4. Kedar Nath Banstola, "Land Revenue Administration In Nepal", (Unpublished Ph.D. Dissertation submitted to the Department of History, Poona), 1985, pp. 280-289.
5. Rostislav Ulyanovsky, *Agrarian India Between the World Wars,* Moscow : Progress Publishers, 1985, pp. 18-19.
6. Robert Eric Frykenberg, *Land Tenure and Peasants In Sourth Asia,* New Delhi : Manohar Publications, 1985, pp. 7-8

to members of the royalty, nobility, aristocracy, and religious propensities or other favourites in the form of *Birta, Guthi,* etc., in which property rights were also handed over. The nature of the rights varied according to the type of tenure. The owners of the *Raikar* tenure registered as tenants in revenue record were required to pay rent and taxes to the state. In fact, the payment to the state is made in lieu of the protection the tenants were entitled to receive.[7] Although the state or rulers transferred ownership rights to individuals through land grants, the grant as such was not absolute. The actual cultivators rented land from landowners and intermediaries and accepted all kinds of financial and other demands from them. The higher concentration of the rural population on the land and the lack of adequate means of production also provided the privileged classes in the agrarian structural hierarchy with the opportunity to make more and more demands. It led to the most deplorable and worst conditions for the peasants until the first half of the twentieth century. The practice of sharecropping, tenants-at-will and fixed rate tenancy were an unbearable burden for cultivators, and were in no way favourable for agricultural development because these forms of tenancies were the worst form of tenancies throughout the regime. The tillers of land were denied of any kind of rights on the land which they cultivated. They could hold land only as long as they paid exorbitant rent and taxes to the landlords. They were also required to satisfy all of their demands and interests. The rate of rent varied from one half to two-thirds of the gross product, which peasants paid to the landowners for continued occupancy of the land. The rate was of course, exorbitant. Under such conditions, the practice of share cropping was more favourable for the cultivators because it, at least provided the opportunity to not owe any rent and one half of the gross produce was retained by the cultivating peasants, known as sharecroppers, in comparison to fixed rate tenancy. But introduction of the

7. W.H. Moreland, *India At The Death of Akbar,* Delhi : Atma Ram & Sons, 1969, p.9.

Kut (payment of product) system in the hill region proved to be a compulsory burden for tenant cultivators. They were compelled to pay fixed rent under all conditions. They were obliged to pay fixed rent even in times of crop failure. No consideration was given in this matter. It had far-reaching economic impact on cultivators and social consequences as well. In fact, an analysis of the entire existing system shows that it was directed against the subsistence interest of the poor cultivators.

In the same way, the Jimidari system made tenants vulnerable. Exploitation by the privileged classes was so great that cultivators were compelled to live under conditions of bare subsistence. In the Eastern Tarai and the *Karnali* region where *Jimindari* system prevailed, the cultivators sometimes could retain only straw, but not grain, because all of the grain was kept by *Jimidars* as rent and as part of interest on loans.[8] Ever since the Shah regime, the agrarian system was profitable only for the privileged classes. No due attention was paid in improving agricultural tenancy by the rulers. There was not even any uniformity in the implementation of existing land laws. Theoretically, it has been proved that the cultivating class lived under most exploited conditions in almost all agrarian societies, because the agrarian system was based on feudal or semi-feudal social systems.[9]

The agrarian system in Nepal during the Rana era had specific features. The traditional land tenure in Nepal had provided the opportunity for the ruling elite to accumulate private wealth. It prepared a basis for the feudal system in the country, and also led to the development of this mode of production in the country.[10] It was characteristic that land was

8. Louis J. Wallinsky, *Selected Papers of Wolf Ladejinsky : Agrarian Reform As An Unfinished Business,* New Your : The World Bank, 1977, pp. 316-323
9. For details see- R.S. Sharma, *Indian Feudalism C 300-1200,* Calcutta : University of Calcutta, 1961, pp. 111-134.
10. Sohan Ram Yadav, *Nepal : Feudalism and Rural Formation,* New Delhi : Cosmo Publications, 1984, p. 19

the property of those who did not till it. On the other hand, the tools of production were in the hands of the cultivators. This opposite situation of divorce between ownership rights and cultivation (with occupancy rights) was most unfavourable for both the peasant economy and agricultural development. The landlords, such as the *Birta* owners, *Jagirdars, Jimidars, Raikar* owners, and others, were very privileged and powerful in their relations with the cultivating community. It tended to continue as a centuries old ruthless exploitation of the toiling peasantry. Even the land holding aristocracy controlled the freedom and lives of peasants. They were forced to obey orders of their lords. The existing feudal mode of production and social system became an important characteristic of Nepal's agricultural system and the status of the owners was part of that system, so, the entire land management system was patterned after the feudal system. Perceval Landon noted -

> *"Prithivi Narayan Shah had created a feudal system of military nature, assessed the revenue to be drawn from each part of the country in a rough but not in unjust manner and left it almost entirely to the feudal overlord to maintain law and order, collect and remit his dues to Kathmandu and execute justice".*[11]

The then agrarian system was most traditional in nature. The insecurity of tenancy, exorbitant rents and numerous customary levies, fragmentation of holdings, increasing rural indebtedness, absence of land rights and status of the peasant community etc. are common problems of traditional agrarian societies.[12] These problems were even common in Nepal before and right after 1951.

---

11. Perceval Landon, *Nepal,* Kathmandu : Ratna Pustak Bhandar, 1976, p. 176
12. H.C.R. Marillat, *Land and Constitution in India,* New York : Columbia University Press, 1979, p. 20.

The Structure of the Agrarian Society :

The basic nature of the agrarian system is reflected in the socio-economic structure of the society. The Food Agriculture Organization document on land reforms and settlement mentions that the structural analysis of an agricultural society reveals agrarian mechanisms and an agro-social structure.[13] The comprehensiveness of the term denotes control, land ownership and use, as well as the interests of various agrarian groups involved in agriculture. It is also related to land holding and modes of production i.e. the feudal mode of production, capitalist mode of production and the Asiatic mode of production.[14] At the same time, the share in agrarian produce, rural indebtedness, and taxation trends are also related to it.[15] Since the term covers a broader meaning, it becomes rather complicated to establish a very strict definition of the term for our purpose in this writing. In spite of differences of opinion, there is a general agreement in the use of the term in a wider sense while referring strictly to farm structures (size of holding) and structures of production, its channelization and the techniques and differing positions of agriculture in the context of varied regions. If social or other aspects are taken into account, the conceptual paradigm of agrarian structure is subordinate to the goals of agricultural policies.[16] Hence one should understand the entire legal and social situation, the constraints of the agrarian community, inter-relations and interdependence as well. Interests of the privileged classes and

13. F.A.O. (ed.), *Land Reforms : Land Settlement & Cooperatives,* Rome : U.N.F.A.O., 1981, p. 6
14. Anthony Brewer, *Marxist Theories of Imperialism.* London : Rouletdge and Kegam Paul, 1989, pp. 28-33 and 40-41.
15. U.N.O., *Land Reforms : Defects in Agrarian Structure As Obstacle to Economic Development,* New York : U.N. Department of Economic Affairs, 1951, pp. 3-4.
16. E.L. Littman, 'The Dynamics of Agrarian Structure in Europe', in U.N.F.A.O. (ed.), *The Dynamics of Agrarian Structure in Europe - WACARD : The Years of Follow Up No. 10* 1978, Rome : U.N.F.A.O., 1988, p. 2.

the rights of ownership and control of the land decisively influence these variables. In this context, it is appropriate to use the term agrarian structure in a slightly different sense. In the context of analysis, the ownership of land and the interpretation of the rights of agrarian communities involved with the land plays vital role. It is appropriate to define and explain the agrarian structure during 1846-1951 in order to acquire in depth knowledge of different aspects of traditional Nepalese agriculture. In fact, agrarian structure in the nineteenth and twentieth centuries was more or less similar to the system of the pre-Rana Shah rule. Although some minor changes were introduced by legal enactment, there were no major attempts to initiate reforms until the promulgation of the Land Reforms Act in 1964. Even after the official declaration of land reforms, some of the defective tenurial features of the Rana era continued to exist. The so called "double ownership" in *Raikar* land, limited tenancy rights, tenurial defects of *Guthi,* the *Kamaiya* system in the form of bonded labour, the *Talukdari* system etc. are examples of such defective tenurial arrangements. In this context, the nature of the use, control and ownership of land remained were almost unchanged in Nepal.[17] Land was exclusively used for two major purposes - firstly to produce yields and secondly for making homestead sites. It was the main source of capital formation and livelihood for the growing population. During the Rana regime, the rights of landowners were absolute in nature. They were the actual beneficiaries of the then agrarian and production relationship and the principal losers were the state on one hand, and the cultivators on the other. The landowners and the land holding intermediaries exacted a large amount as their share in the form of rent and levies, whereas some of them paid a nominal amount to the state. Even during the 1950's, tax assessment based on productivity (*adhiyan=half*) took no account of changes in the market price of commodities. Although the price of grain

---

17. Mahesh Chandra Regmi, *Thatched Huts and Stucco Palaces,* New Delhi : Vikas Publishing House, 1978, p. 107-120.

changed, the system of channelization remained unchanged and that increased the incomes of the privileged classes. Even though the share of the privileged classes increased significantly, the share of the state remained unchanged. Therefore, the state was the principal looser in the then agricultural system due to the channelization of gross agrarian produce.

The data pertaining to agrarian activities, the structure, and analysis of the existing situation is insufficient. Even the historical data on the farm structure, farm population's income, the size of holdings etc. have not been properly analysed. Due to this situation, some of the available statistical data are analyzed in appropriate places. The inadequacy of statistical data has led to hypothetical analysis of the historical facts regarding the structure of Nepalese agrarian society, agrarian production relations, tenurial conditions and so on.

Table No-1

Share in agrarian produce by various groups in - 1950s.

	Central Tarai	Eastern Tarai	Bhaktapur	Kathmandu
Land type	*Birta*	*Jimindari*	*Raikar (Abal)*	*Pota Birta*
Total Production	24 Mounds (Rs.420)	30 Mounds	6 Mounds Rs.105	6 Mounds Rs.105
Rent Levied	12Mounds. Rs210	20 Mounds	4 Mounds Rs.70	4 Mounds Rs.70
State's Share	4 Mounds Rs. 70	0.75 Mounds (2.5 %)	0.81 Mounds Rs. 6.52 (13.5%)	0.084 Mounds Rs. 0.50 (1.4%)
Owners' +Holders' share	8 Mds Rs. 140 (66.3 %)	29..25 Mds (97.5 %)	5.19 Mounds Rs.63.48 (86.5%)	5.92 Mounds Rs.69.50 (98.67%)

— In Jimidari land in Jhapa, the Jimidars exacted almost all grain in the form of rent, taxes and interest on loans / Source: Wallinsky, f.n.8, p. 316

The following table depicts data on the share of gross crops claimed by various agrarian groups. It is clear that for all taxable land, the state's share in agricultural product was incredibly low in comparison to the share of the individual landowners. This table makes it clear that the state had been the principal loser in sharing agrarian income, although it was the ultimate proprietor of all of the land.

This table shows that in all cases, tenants paid two-third of the gross crop as rent. It excludes the customary taxes and exorbitant interest on loans which the landowners and landholders were entitled to collect. The surplus production was exacted by the landowners, so the cultivating peasants could retain little of it. Their responsibility to invest in order to initiate cultivation also left them in bare subsistence conditions. The share of the state was nominal in all tenures. The highest percentage share of the state was 13.5 % of the total rent exacted in Awal-Raikar in Bhaktapur area, but on the contrary, the landowners and intermediaries retained a handsome amount. This system of channelization of production was not profitable for the state, at least not in economic terms; however, the ruling elite had political benefits. Needless to say this system was also unfavourable for cultivators and other tenants to increase production. The landowning class had not any kind of material or financial obligations to assist in the production process. Neither they were required to play any role to improve agricultural tenancy or made investment necessary in order to diversify the rural economy. In fact, it was not necessary for them because they regularly received the stipulated rent within the required time frame as agreed upon by the cultivators even under the most unfavourable conditions. The peasant cultivators were required to pay grain at the place where landowners desired. The rent in tenures other than the Raikar was determined primarily by population density and the constant pressure on land. The owners of such land were permitted to bid on land for cultivation. This is the reason why the amount of rent varied to some extent from one place to another. The higher pressure on the land provided an opportunity for bidding. The quantity of rent collected in different areas was two- thirds in Mahottari, one-third in Kailali-Kanchanpur, and two-thirds on the best land in the central hill region during the first half of the twentieth century. But sometimes, competition to obtain land for cultivation also affected the appropriation of rent.[18] There was no attempt to reform such unregulated rent and taxes throughout the country.[19] It was only after the promulgation of the Land Act of 1957 that the payment of rent was fixed at the rate of one half of the gross crop.[20] But this "Land settlement" did not affect the customary practices which were generally less than one half of the gross product. The new law restricted owners or intermediaries from increasing rent beyond the ceiling. Later in 1958 the rent was reduced to one-third.[21] Both of the laws were proved to be most significant rescue measures for the toiling cultivators. The rent was regulated for the first time in the country's history, but sharecropping tenancy still continued to exist, and arbitrarily fixed the rent at one half of the gross product.

The land holding aristocracy during the Rana regime, did not give any incentive to increase production and improve tenancy, which would later benefit both the parties involved in agriculture. But the situation was not favourable for the peasantry. The cultivators were compelled to only produce a quantity of crops which was adequate to pay the compulsory rent, taxes and for their own subsistence. Any increase in production automatically increased the amount of rent. Therefore, they were not very eager to invest, labour and capital to increase production, because it was not profitable for them. In fact, they needed to borrow capital from moneylenders to invest which was, by no means desirable to them. The growing rural indebtedness and

---

18. Mahesh Chandra Regmi, *Land Tenure & Taxation In Nepal,* Kathmandu : Ratna Pustak Bhandar, 1978, pp. 14-15
19. Different types of taxes are found rpeatedly referred in the historical documents. There are more than 360 types of taxes and levies counted so far during this research. See appendix. 6
20. 'Bhumi Sambandhi *Ain*-2014 V.S. :, (Land Act 1975), *Nepal Kanun Patrika,* Vol. VI, No. 8, 2018 B.S., Kathmandu : The Supreme Court, pp. 192-98, also see : Nepal Gazettee, pt. V, No. 5, 22 Shrava, 2014.
21. *Ibid,*.

lack of money compelled them to contract debts with the moneylenders and agree to pay exorbitant rates of interest. In this case, it was even possible for them to invest capital in order to improve agriculture. Both cultivation and the peasants' household economy were interconnected with the rent. The peasants paid exorbitant rates of levies, taxes and rent without protesting in order to avoid displeasing the landlords and intermediaries. The fear of eviction played an important role in the peasant economy too. As a rule, the burden of rent and taxes under the Rana rule fell on the most impoverished and proletarian peasants, but comparatively prosperous peasants shifted their part of the burden of cultivation and the payment of rent, taxes and levies to subtenants and sharecroppers by letting land to them for cultivation almost on a sharecropping basis.[22] In this situation, the subtenants were the ones who agreed to fulfill all kinds of obligations. The political and economic status of absentee and resident landowners and intermediaries and their power in the agrarian structural hierarchy made these terms unfavourable and conjured up images of rich absentee landlords or oppressive local bosses exacted exorbitant rent from the cultivators of the land.[23] In fact, they had been synonymous with the ruthless exploitation of Nepalese peasants. It was similar to the situation for which Karl Marx had described the theory of class struggle.[24] The economic conditions of the peasantry compelled them to till the land without rights. There were various groups in the hierarchy, which safeguarded the interests of the land owning elite. The elite group also had protection and was supported through the fulfillment of interests. A similar system also existed in British India.[25] The actual cultivators were prevented from having direct relations with the state with the exception of the owner-cultivators

22. Ulyanovsky, f.n. 5, pp. 127-128.
23. Merillat, f.n. 12, p. 19.
24. Harold J. Laski, *The Communist Manifesto-Socialist Landmark*, London : George Allen and Unwin, 1961, pp. 119-122.
25. F.A.O.-I.L.O, *Progress In Land Feforms*, New York : U.N.O., 1976, p. 50.

of the *Raikar* land who were registered as rent-paying tenants in revenue record. The district revenue record contained only their names as taxpayers, but it did not mention the names of the actual cultivators; in fact, it virtually ignored them. This situation always played an important role in determining the agrarian relations of that time. The activities and status of different rungs in the hierarchy were determined by their caste as well their social and economic status, powers and family connections. The hunger for land of the rural poor also accelerated the influx of various interests. Growing rural unemployment, the lack of adequate land for cultivation, the abundant supply of agricultural labour, the association of landowners with the ruling community, and the traditional Hindu-culture determined the status of cultivators and the peasant economy. This was the situation which compelled the peasant community to be content with defective tenure arrangements, such as the traditional type of tenancy, share cropping, service tenures (*Rakam* and *Jhara*), the payment of *Koshelees* (gifts) and other financial burdens.

The existing tenurial conditions and the agrarian system showed that land ownership involved relatively in a small percentage of the population, whereas the majority of the rural population was either landless labourers, tenants, sub-tenants, sharecroppers, or agricultural serfs. Thus, the privileged classes were few in number, but dominated the large mass of peasant cultivators. The *Muluki* Ain and its subsequent amendments dealt with the agrarian system and other related topics, but there was not even one single attempt to improve agricultural tenancy. The existing system had given unlimited rights to the gentry. The absentee landlords held vast areas of cultivable land, mostly in the Tarai, under their control and enjoyed extra judicial power within their jurisdiction. The big landlords were given additional power, which included judicial power and tax collecting rights.[26] The government itself was determined to safeguard those

26. Rajya grant to Raja Jaya Pritihvi Bhadur Singh 1960 V.S., Poka. 38, Duciment no 26, Kathmandu : Record Section of the Depatment of Revenue HMG Nepal.

privileges which had been given to the landowning elite. This kind of situation in Rana Nepal is similar to the situation in Chhotanagpur under the British rule in India.[27] The cultivators in both the places were always subordinate to the will of the landowners and intermediaries.

The agrarian system throughout the century was marked by inequalities in the size of holdings. A small minority of upper class citizens controlled a substantial portion of agricultural land. It provided a favourable environment for controlling both the economy and the population there by strengthening the elite's political control. But on the other hand, millions of rural poor people were subjected to numerous abuses and weighed down by the contemporary economic structure, perpetual indebtedness, and eked out a precarious existence on tiny fragmented holdings while utilizing outdated farming practices. The peasants were placed at the lowest rung of the hierarchy and their economy was ruined. The absentee landlords enjoyed property rights in land and this situation gave rise to another class of people in agrarian society who were, for all intents and purposes, the non-cultivating intermediaries. This group of people acted on behalf of the absentees by managing land,

---

— Rajya grant to Bhirkot Raja Lalit Bahadur 1925 V.S., Poka no. 2, Record Section of The Department of Revenue HMG, Nepal.

— 'Judicial Powers of Birta Owners and Jagirdars', *Regmi Research Series* Year - 8, No. 2, Feb. 1976 Kathmandu : Regmi Research Institute, 1976, pp. 25-32, and *Regmi Research Series,* Year 8, no 3 March 1976, p-53.

On Raja Title of Galkot Raja Prithvi Bam Malla 1925 V.S. Poka no 2, Record Section of the Department of Revenue HMG, Nepal.

Land Grrant to Raja of Bajura 1960 V.S., Poka no 159, Jaishi Kotha documents no 29, 30 and 34, Kathmandu : Record Section of the Department of Revenue HMG, Nepal.

27. Suresh Singh, The Munda Land System and Revenue Reforms In Chhotanagpur During 1869-1908', in Ram Sharan Sharma (ed.) *Land Revenue In India,* New Delhi : Moti Lal Banarasi Dass, 1971, p. 107.

collecting rent and levies and, at the same time, they further increased the wealth and served the interests of their masters.

The agrarian structure in Rana Nepal was more or less similar to the system that prevailed during the Shah period (1768-1846). No radical changes took place which could have led to overall reforms in the structure. All productive activities which were initiated by cultivators were self sustained without outside support, but the bulk of the benefit that was derived from their labour went to the purses of the landed aristocracy. The economic interests of the involved parties collided and were often in conflict. The economic inequalities aggravated the social and political disturbances. Although a well defined land policy was lacking throughout the Rana regime, the rulers' interests led them to protect the interests of the land holding aristocracy through the issuing of various *Rukkas* (orders), Sanads (covering rights), *Sawals* (regulations) and *Hukums* (royal verdicts). The Rana premiers issued these kinds of orders on different occasions. In certain cases, such orders also contradicted each other. This was a common practice in the Rana administration. In all cases, it favoured the landed aristocracy. All the social groups in Nepal were connected to the land in one way or another. A large portion of the population was engaged in agrarian activities. Almost 70 % of Asia's population engaged in agrarian activities. The relationship of population to land has been one of the most important features of Nepal's agrarian structure.

The following table 2 compares relationship of population to land in some Asian countries.[28]

This table contains data on the relationship of population to land in different countries. Although the data on Nepal was collected during 1953-54, it provides a basis for discussing the agrarian situation in Nepal before 1951. The per capita hector in Nepal was higher than that of Japan, Afghanistan and Sri Lanka. One half of the total area in Nepal was cultivable but only one-fourth was cultivated and the remaining portion was left uncultivated.

28. U.N.O., f.n. 15, p. 96

Table No. 2
Relation of Population to Land

Country & Year	Population (000)	Area Hec. (000)	Cultivable Land		Per Capita Hec
			% of Total Area	% of Total Area	
Nepal 1953-4	9385	1927	50	50	0.22
Afghanistan 947	12000	1150	1.8	—	0.10
Burma 1947	18489	8754	14.6	60.8	0.47
India 1947	346000	98696	43.8	58.7	0.27
Japan 1948	83196	5907	16.1	68.5	0.07
Pakistan 1948	74437	21100	22.6	70.0	0.28
Sri Lanka 1950	7539	1315	20.0	50.0	0.1

Even since the Shah regime, various land tenures were regulated. During the Rana regime, land tenure remained intact. Only after the end of the totalitarian Rana regime, were some of the defective and traditional tenures abolished; this was primarily aimed at reforming in the existing land tenure, tenurial conditions, existing feudal systems, and so on. Even since 1957, the series of legal enactment was basically intended to give little incentive to those producers who had been ruthlessly exploited for centuries. The end of some of the tenures converted it into Raikar land. Later, the promulgation of the Land Act in 1964 brought about perceptible changes in both the peasant economy and the existing agrarian social structure of the country. During that time, all of the land was divided into various tenures. There were altogether seven tenures, such as- *Raikar, Birta, Jagir, Rakam, Rajya, Kipat* and *Guthi*. They covered altogether 19,27,000 hector of land.[29]

29. *Wallinsky,* f.n. 8, pp. 316-323.

Almost one half of the land was Raikar. It was followed by Birta tenure. In Birta, the proprietary right was given to individuals. Although a vast expanse of land (almost 86 %) was covered by these two tenure. The remaining tenures, such as Jagir, Rakam, Rajya, Kipat and Guthi, were small in area. All tenures except Guthi have already been abolished. In Nepal the state is still the ultimate proprietor of land, so it had every right and authority to demand a share in agrarian produce in the form of rent and taxes. The pattern of land holding is also important in discussing agrarian relations or agrarian social structure. For example, some of the statistical data on land holding in a village in Morang can be presented here for better understanding of the situation. In one of the villages in Morang before 1950, the problem of landlessness had grown acute. Almost one half of the agrarian families (50.40 %) were landless labourers, so they were compelled to survive only by these means. One fourth (23.10 %) of the families held less than one bigha of land. The rest of the families, comprising 26.50 % held more than one bigha of land.

The data shows the percentage of land ownership held by the members of peasant community. The data is alarming due to the fact that peasants were compelled to fulfill all the demands of the owners and intermediaries; otherwise the poor peasants were deprived of land. The Land Commission in Bardia (1952) also reported a similar trend of land ownership. The large-scale owners were relatively small in number whereas a large percentage of the rural population held small and fragmented holdings. Furthermore, one half of the rural families were landless agristic serfs. The excessively large estates were few in number, the middle sized estates were numerous, and the small estates were countless.[30]

As a matter of fact, the pattern of land ownership in that society favoured the aristocracy. The "Bardia Land Commission" also reported that large scale landlords owned

30. N.M. Pal, *Some Social and Economic Aspects of Bengal,* Calcutta : The Book Company, 1926, pp. 21-22.

24,000 *Bighas* and small sized owners held 56,000 *Bighas* in 1910 in Bardia district. This situation had been reversed by 42 years, later in 1952. Similarly, the land occupied by peasants decreased from 80% to 25% within a period of fifteen years (1893-1908) in the western Tarai. This situation deteriorated further due to growing rural indebtedness and *vice versa*, and became an acute agrarian problem in the country. The landowners controlled vast areas of land under their proprietorship. Most of the large scale landowners were absentees. The holdings of Prime Minister Mathbar Singh Thapa, for an instance, consisted of 25,346 *bighas* in the Tarai and 1,797. 5 *Muri* of land in the hills. In addition to that, he received Rs. 117,475 per annum. At the same time, he was also entitled to exact 12,401 Rs. from his Khuwa villages and rice lands.[31] This was the common trend among the high-class families.[32]

The economic potential of the landowning class was necessarily associated with the political power. In agrarian societies, the landowners' interests are accommodated by the political system, thus forming a dominant position in the society. Their needs were met by exacting surplus production. It is obvious that economy has remained subordinate to politics throughout history.[33] The interest of various groups in the land involve rights and duties, and that many of these may exist with respect to the same physical piece of land property. The prevailing agrarian structure has a profound impact in the national economy as well. The existing economic structure

31. 'Birta Grant to Mathbar Singh Thapa', *Regmi Research Series,* Year 8, No. 3, March 1976, Kathmandu : Regmi R esearch Institute, pp. 46-49.
32. 'Farmaisi Brita Grant to Khaga Raj Dibyaswori' 1964 V.S., Poka-38, S.No. 3797, Kathmandu : Record Section of the Department of Revenue.

    The total Area was 616 *Bighas* in Morang and 930 *Bighas* in Kathbana area. It was granted (as *Farmaisi Birta*) for priv purse.
33. Ian Roxborough. *Thories of Underdevelopment,* London : Mac Millian Company, 1979, pp. 2-5

caused the toiling peasantry to remain subject to most vulnerable conditions.

The agrarian structure in Nepal (1846-1951) had specific features that can be explained in the following terms. The pattern of land control was very traditional in nature and governed the entire agrarian system. In spite of the state's absolute land rights, a small number of nobility, aristocracy and bureaucrats controlled large areas of cultivable land, in comparison to the higher percentage of landless rural population, which had no means of production. Along with the means of production, the privileged classes even controlled the lives of the cultivating community. This had been a distinct characteristic of the land system in Nepal. There were no favourable conditions to motivate the rural work force and economy. Therefore, the rural poor were compelled to rely on the land for survival. It finally resulted in a high rate of rural indebtedness and inter regional migration. The then conditions of the Nepalese peasants and cultivators compelled them to borrow money and grain from rich landlords and moneylenders. Usually, the moneylenders were the landlords. It was serious problem in Nepal during that period, statistical data relating to of rural indebtedness is not available.

The entire population fit into the agrarian social structure without racial distinctions. The state, as a landlord, occupied the upper most position. It was the ultimate proprietor of all land and its rights were absolute. The landowners and intermediaries shared rights with the state. During the Rana regime, there existed a stratified agrarian society in which land rights and mutual economic relations between classes were inextricably linked to the power and prerogatives of the sovereign and his agents. The agrarian-social hierarchical structure as such was complex in nature. In the hierarchy of rights of people and classes in terms of ownership, occupancy, management or cultivation of land, the gathering and disposing of its produce and the collection and appropriation of rent which was due on account of the land, the first place was occupied by the government which claimed a share of the agricultural produce as land revenue. However, the amount of state's share was insignificant in all taxable tenures. This situation continued even after 1951 in the Raikar system, in which tenancy occurred.

The structural hierarchy of agrarian communities merits discussion. The hierarchy and structure in nineteenth and twentieth century Nepal was as shown in the chart (appendix No. 1).

The agrarian communities illustrated in the diagram enjoyed various rights and privileges according to their status in the hierarchy. The relationship that emerged between different groups from time to time was unequal. The landowners generally held proprietary and property rights, but the actual cultivators were denied any land rights. This kind of system continued even after 1951, and was reflected in land laws and royal proclamations issued before 1964. The political economists of Nepal have agreed upon the theory of the "Triple system" in agrarian relations, which influenced the entire agrarian system in the country. Of course, the state had kept other parties in balance and continued its administration. The landowners provided credit in the form of debt for cultivation, whereas the cultivators supplied labour and initiated production.[34] But one should realize that the inflow of capital from the landowners was never a part of their duty rather it was a business practice which was lucrative for them.

The Agrarian Hierarchies and Relationship Patterns: The State As The Ultimate Proprietor :

In fact, it is an Asian indigenous system that made the state the biggest landlord. So, its place in the hierarchical structure is always at the top. The proprietary right is also vested in the State.

So, it is the ultimate holder of all land, cultivated or uncultivated. It controlled all types of land even when land

34. *Report of The Land Revenue Commission of Bengal,* Calcutta : Government of Bengal, 1940, pp. 5-6

rights were shared with individuals on various occasions. When the state becomes the controller of agrarian relationships, an enormous administrative structure with a bureaucratic agency is required. To deal directly and efficiently with the cultivators, the Rana government thus formed a network of official and unofficial functionaries in rural areas of Nepal. As land rights in land were vested in the state, it had every right to grant land to the individuals, officials, religious organizations and charitable institutions in the form of *Birta, Jagir, Guthi* and *Rakam* tenures. Thus, a large area came under private ownership. In some cases, the state transferred ownership rights through financial transactions also. Even under such conditions, the state itself held proprietary rights and the right to control the land. Similarly, it secured the right to confiscate land. Before 1951, the peasants as a group of people were hardly important for the state because it was not they who paid revenue to the government,[35] therefore, the state made no attempts to reform tenancy, tenurial conditions or overall conditions for the cultivators. Those interests necessarily involved increasing financial gain by oppressing the peasants through various means. The *Ain* of 1910 V.S. (1854 AD) and its subsequent amendments in 1886 and 1935 A.D. explained the role of the state as a landlord, and protected the rights and privileges of the state.[36] It had right to alienate it through sale, mortgage, bequest and so on. The division of rights between the state and individuals had been one of the most important features of the contemporary agrarian system. The state granted property right to the *Birta* owners. They were permitted to transfer rights through lease, sale, mortgage or inheritance. The Raikar tenure holders acquired such rights only after the beginning of the twentieth century.[37] The *Raikar* tenants were also provided with

35. Mahesh Chandrra Regmi. *Land Ownership In Nepal,* Berkeley : University of California Press, 1976, pp. 194-96.
36. *Sir 5 Surendra Bikram Shah Ko Pala Ma Baneko Muluki Ain* (The Civil Code Enancted During the Reign of King Surendra Bikram Shah), Kathmandu : Ministry of Law and Jusitce, 2022 V.S., pp. 1-52.
37. Regmi, f.n. 18, pp. 754-755

occupancy rights but the transfer of such rights was not permitted. There were no private property rights in *Raika*r, but the owners that is the registered tenants, were authorized to exact rent and taxes from cultivators which was usually fixed according to the lease contract or statute and which was no less than one half of the gross product. The land property rights allow one to exercise one's own will with respect to the land, and this right is non-existent unless there is at least some opportunity to use and enjoy it where one has free will.[38] The landowners were required to pay certain amounts as revenue to the state, but they were not given transaction rights.[39] Later on, limited occupancy rights were agreed upon and sub-infeudation was permitted. It led to the creation of an active role in Nepalese agriculture for land holding intermediaries. The occupants also rented land for cultivation rather than cultivating by themselves. During the course of time, the laws made the *Raikar* a commodity, which could easily be sold or purchased on the agrarian market, but the state always enjoyed unlimited rights in *Raikar* in terms of use and occupancy as the ultimate proprietor of land property.

The cultivators with occupancy right were permitted to till the land as long as they paid rent and taxes regularly as prescribed either by statute or custom, but cultivators without occupancy rights were considered tenants-at-will or the *Magani* tenants. During the latter half of the regime, the *Raikar* occupants also began investing in land. In 1886, a law permitted the transfer of occupancy right involving money with prior approval of the local *Talukdars*. The land owners relied on appropriation of surpluses in the form of rent and taxes. The right of tax collection granted to them by the government was aimed at keeping law and order intact and maintaining the trails and ferries, without which

38. 'Jagga Jamin Ko Mahal', (Proposition of Rules Relating To The Land), *The Muluki Ain 1945* V.S., Vol. III, Kathmandu : Government of Nepal.
39. *Ibid.*

communication and transportation would have been impossible in the mountains.[40]

The state collected rent in kind through the intermediaries. It had created manifold problems, including the construction of warehouses, transportation etc.

The Asian system of state landlordism created various drawbacks in land holding.[41] It was the traditional form of land ownership in Nepal but the interests of the landlords were in conflict with those of other groups in the society. The concept and creation of rights according to state landlordism had not produced progressive agriculture, indeed it had been impoverishing the peasantry.[42] By statute and tradition, land has been the property of the state. By virtue of traditional land practice, property rights in land could be confiscated by the state in Nepal and the state retained this power and thus held absolute rights to collect rent, confiscate or hand over rights to individuals. The cultivators did not pay directly to the state but paid through landowners or intermediaries. The land system thus constituted the medium through which agricultural production was channelized to satisfy the state, landowners, and land holding intermediaries, religious organizations, and others. This system made it so that surplus production belonged to the state, which shared it with the aristocratic and bureaucratic groups.[43]

The role of the peasantry until 1951 and later was limited to providing surplus production as rent, levies and taxes upon which the ruling aristocracy relied. During this period, the methods of appropriation of the surplus were strengthened.[44] It made the peasant community merely an instrument with which

40. David Seddan, *et.al, Peasants And Workers In Nepal,* New Delhi : Vikas Publishing House, 1979, pp. 21-23.
41. Sulekh Chandra Gupta, *Agrarian Relation and British Rule In India,* Bombay : Asia Publishing House, 1963, p. x.
42. *Ibid.*
43. Regmi, f.n. 17, pp. 53-69.
    — Ulyanovsky, f.n. 5, pp. 108-148.
44. Seddan, *et.al,* f.n. 40, pp. 48-50

to produce surplus production. The state's role was always that of a large-scale landlord.

The Land Owners :

The landowners and land holding intermediaries were the most favoured classes in the Nepalese agrarian setup. The landowners and landholders denote both the absentees and resident landowners. The intermediary tenants were always involved between the owners and cultivators. They were the upper class, with various land privileges. Thus, they ruled over the peasantry. They were also divided into various sub-types. Those different types are automatically included while discussing major types or otherwise specified in the analysis in the context of their privileges, rights and duties.

In agrarian society, this class of people enjoyed all land rights. Hypothetically, if one man an absolute master and the sole owner of all the land and all other men are his slaves, the system of justice, peace, security and tranquility which he established are such that it necessarily brought satisfaction to most of his people.[45] Of course, at least we did not find any protest against this hypothesis in Nepal before 1950 from the lower rung of the agrarian hierarchy even under the most unfavourable conditions. It was only after the activities of the Marxist leaders that the peasants gradually overcome their ignorance and stood against all kinds of exploitation, which was contrary to their interests.

Basically, the absentees, resident owners and land holding intermediaries belonged to that class, who constituted major force in the traditional agrarian system. Their authority was imposed under the traditional land system. The Civil Code of 1854 favoured that class very much, but its subsequent amendments began to create conditions which were somewhat favourable for the cultivators although insignificantly. So, later on it led to the emergence and growth of peasants' land rights. As mentioned earlier, the privileged classes did not play any

45. Frykenberg, f.n. 6, p. 4.

role in the production process; it was sufficient for them to be the owners and to exercise all kinds of powers and privileges. The excessively high rate of rural indebtedness, the traditional system of credit supply, exorbitant interest rates, the moneylender's monopoly and association of money lending with land ownership provided favourable conditions for the privileged classes. The customary practice that a cultivator should not be evicted as long as he agreed to pay rent was the only incentive to initiate production. The peasants had no significant land rights but later on they were permitted to inherit and divide property in the Raikar which they occupied. It was a landmark in the evolution of cultivators' rights on Raikar land, which later proved to be significant. Gradually, they began long-term possession and transfer of occupancy rights in exchange for monetary payment.[46]

The landowners deserved higher ranks in the hierarchy of agrarian society. The large scale *Birta, Jagir*, and *Guthi* owners were absentee landlords whereas small scale owners resided in villages. The legal and economic status of the landowners made them very powerful in rural societies. The *Birta* owners in general had no financial obligations towards the state, but the resident landowners often initiated cultivation by themselves. Both the resident owners and intermediaries worked on behalf of the absentees and they provided also a non-institutional source of credit in the villages which was easily accessible to peasants living in and around those areas. The landlords in villages enjoyed various rights and privileges, including the dispensing of justice.[47] The *Muluki Ain* of 2012 V.S. (1955

46. Regmi, f.n. 17, p. 108
47. Powers and privileges were usually mentioned in the land grant.
    — *Lal Mohars* (documents with the royal red seal).
    — *Birta grant to Gulami Raja,* f.n. 26.
    — *Rajya grant to Gulmi Raja Chiranjibi Bikram Shah 1992* V.S., Record Section of the Department of Revenue HMG Nepal.
    — *Daijo Birta Grant to the Daughter of HRH Maharaja since Basathi Sal 1963* V.S., Poka No. 42, Record Section of the Department of Revenue HMG, Nepal.

A.D) also mentioned the power and authority of the absentee landlords. They were also authorized to hear legal suits in their areas. Some limitations, however, were imposed on such hearings.[48] In fact, their powers and privileges were a form of political or socio-economic authority and control. At the same time, the intermediaries also enjoyed multiple economic benefits. The power and position of the privileged classes ultimately contributed to the strengthening of the feudal setup of the agrarian economy in the Rana period. But there was a system according to which the resident landowners cultivated the absentees' land in the capacity of a cultivator. In this case, he had to fulfill all other obligations as a cultivator. There were no legal restrictions imposed on them for such practices. This practice made them landowners and cultivating tenants at the same time, although they were required to fulfill the duties of a tenant in relation to the landlords. Their previous status as influential landowners was never affected, they tended to continue to played significant role in the agrarian relationship in the capacity of landowners.

The introduction of the Kut system, or fixed rate tenancy in the hills provided them with a net income status. Although there was a lack of incentives to raise production, the cultivators had to produce adequate grain both for payment of the Kut, and for themselves. The absentee landlords lived far away from their land. It was impractical for them to live in villages due to political and socio-economic factors, so, they depended solely on intermediaries to manage their holdings. Kirkpatrick thus noted:

> *"Though one or two men might, if time allowed, plough a Kaith (land) very well, yet as several*

— *Rajya Birta Grant to Bhirkot Raja Lalit Bahadur 1925* V.S., Poka no. 2, Record Section of the Department of Revenuw, HMG, Nepal.

— Also see : Akhtar, f.n. 1, pp. 90-114 and 170-278.

48. *The Muluki Ain* Vol. I (The Civil Code), Kathmandu : Gorkhapatra Press, 2012 V.S. pp. 151-157.

> *hands are required to sow and reap it. There can be a small proportion of it separately managed by the Jaghiredar or occupier, however numerous his family may be. He generally, therefore satisfies himself with cultivating a few Moories in which he usually raises fruits or vegetables, leaving the rest to the Mohi (tenant) or undertaker (intermediaries) with whom he engages."*[49]

The prevailing agricultural conditions and their social status compelled the absentees to depend on intermediaries to look after their land, but resident landowners lived in their respective villages and had a direct link with the production process. The local landowners had more chances to accumulate wealth by various means than the absentees. They used surplus rent in money lending, the acquisition of land, reclamation, the improvement of irrigation facilities and trade in agricultural products.[50] The surplus rent was related to the deterioration of the rural economy. But the large part of capital collected from villages was not spent in those areas. The rural capital was generally transferred to towns. In such a condition, the resident owners were the only source of credit supply in villages.[51] This situation remained in practice throughout the century long Rana rule, but only after 1964 was the amount that was retained in local areas increased, because the statute reduced the rent and increased the cultivators' share. The regime also attempted to maintain the continuity of old traditions in order to mobilize political support and finance the civil and military administration.[52] This policy of the Ranas guided the entire land policy administration as well as the functioning of traditional land tenure system.

49. William Kirkpatrick, *An Account of The Kingdom of Nepal,* New Delhi : Manju Shree Publishing House, 1969, p. 98
50. Regmi, f.n. 17, p. 39
51. Bal Krishna Pokharel, *Panch Saya Varsha* (Five Hundred Years). Lalitpur : Jagadamba Prakashan, 2031 B.S., pp. 383-86.
52. Regmi, f.n. 17, pp. 40-41

Land holding Intermediaries :

The other privileged class in the agrarian hierarchy was the community of land holding intermediaries. They acted in between the owners and cultivators. They were an essential part of Nepal's agrarian system. The intermediary character of their work had given them various powers and privileges to enjoy. In and around the hills of Kathmandu, the government appointed Mohi Naikes (intermediary tenants) giving them every possible right in order to deal with the Raikar and Jagera (surplus) land tenants. An office known as the Mohi Naike Bandovasta Adda (the office dealing with the intermediary tenants) was established accordingly.

Francis Buchanan Hamilton has noted-.

> *"Landholders (intermediaries and sometimes owners) who do not cultivate ... estate, in general let them for one half of the grain produced."*[53]

In ancient times, land owned by Brahmins, charitable institutions and religious organizations was cultivated by peasants, and owners enjoyed various benefits. All such land was tax exempt. The intermediaries collected rent from peasants on behalf of the landowners while retaining a portion of it for themselves. This was the same case with the *Jagirdars* in India.[54] The practice in India thus, created an intermediary land group. Kautilya, in his *Arthashastra* (The Economics), mentioned that land should be given to peasants by the king and not by such intermediaries.[55] This clearly shows how powerful they were. Perhaps Kautilya aimed at eradicating the intermediaries' role

53. Frnacis Buchnan Hmailton, *An Account of The Kingdom of Nepal And of Terriroties Annexed By The House of Gorkha,* New Delhi : Mnaju shree Publishing House, 1971, p. 220
54. Ram Sharan Sharma, *Lights On Early History and Economy,* Calcutta : P.C. Manaktala & Sons, 1966, p. 2.
55. R. Shamashastry, *Kautiliya Artha Shastra,* Mysore : Raghuveer Printing Press, 1924, pp. 1-4.

in the land holding system, which made no contribution to the production process. Similarly, Yagnavalkya introduced a three tier hierarchy in the agrarian structure- the *Mahipati* (the king), *Kshetra Swami* (landowner) and *Krishaka* (farmer).[56] He also ignored the intermediaries in the land holding practice. At that time, the *Kshetra Swami* (owner of land) leased out land to peasants. They were liable to be punished if they neglected or failed to cultivate but during the course of time, the intermediaries became an essential part of the land holding system. They provided a base for developing feudalism in agrarian societies.[57] In ancient India, the intermediaries imposed rent and numerous taxes such as *Udranga* (frontier tax), *Uparikara* (tribute to the divisional officers) and *Hiranya* (tax in cash) which they collected from the cultivators.

In Nepal, this group of intermediaries emerged due to the existing laws, tenurial policies, and agrarian conditions that prevailed in the country. In India in the middle of the seventeenth century, the great bulk of revenue, as much as 190,000,000 out of 220,000,000 was assigned and consequently the assignees were the intermediaries.[58] Virtually all of the bonded peasants lived in terrible poverty and ignorance. The intermediary exacted the surplus production. The upper most structure of the agrarian relations was thus created, and served the immediate needs of the rulers and the landed aristocracy. By the end of the Rana rule, this class structure was comprised of revenue receiving intermediaries, rent receiving intermediaries, and the owner-cultivators, who remained powerful and dominant in the agrarian economy.[59]

56. Girija Prasad Dwivedi, *Yagnavalkya Smriti,* Lucknow : Nawal Kishore, 1915, pp. 39-40.
57. Sharma, f.n. 9, pp. 210-262
58. W.H. Mooreland, *Agrarian Structure of Muslim India,* Allahabad : Central Book Depot, 1929, p. 150
59. Nav Raj Chalise, 'Land Tennure And Tennacy in Neal', in -*Report of National Seminar On Land Reform,* Kathmandu : Ministry of Land Reforms, 1970, p. 39

In Nepal, the primary aim of the Rana administration was to collect revenue and maintain law and order. Therefore, the state machinery enforced royal decrees on tenurial grants. If anybody opposed the state's policy, they were supposed to be punished by confiscation of their property and even by capital punishment.[60] The landowners and intermediaries assisted the government in promoting land reclamation and developing settlements. The *Jetha-raiyat* represented the peasant community while dealing with intermediaries in the Tarai, and gained higher prestige among the peasants. They also existed in the Kathmandu valley. Their equivalent was the *Budhyauli*, who dealt with the *Kipatiya Subbas* and the privileged classes in Limbuwan (Eastern Nepal). On some occasions, the intermediaries were responsible for land allotment, revenue collection and dispensing justice at the local level on behalf of the landowners. But the abolition of the intermediaries after the end of the Ranas' rule proved to be a good step toward improving the conditions of the peasantry, because this practice was never favourable for agricultural development. The intermediary practice was common in *Jagir, Birta*, Guthi and to some extent in Raikar, whereas the local revenue functionaries in general dealt with cultivators in *Raikar, Kipat* and *Rakam* tenures. But in some instances, intermediaries were also found practice in these tenures. The *Talukdars Jimidars, Jimmawals* (on rice field), Mukhiya (on dry land), Choudhary, Patwari and others were all intermediaries who were active in different parts of the country. The intermediaries enjoyed various rights and privileges. Therefore, the intermediary's job was an attractive one to many people. Their rights varied according to time and place, but their basic role did not change for centuries. They were very active in *Jimidari* (in the Eastern *Tarai* and *Karnali* region), *Birta* and *Jagir* tenures. In the *Jimidari* tenure, the *Jimidar* and *Chuni* were main categories

60. Tulasi Ram Vaidya and Tri Ratna Manandhar, *Crime and Punishment In Nepal,* Kathmandu : Purna and Bini, 1985, pp. 195-207.

of intermediaries. A *Jimidar* were very influential and powerful in their areas and controlled the entire population under their jurisdiction.[61] Thus, they became masters of large areas.[62] This system itself was a part of the means of ensuring a constant flow of income.[63]

There was little difference in the *Jimdari* and *Zamindari* systems. The term *Zamindar* historically denoted to the land owning class. The possessor of *Zamindari* rights did not posses visible articles of property, like the others but instead held a title and received a constant share of the gross produce.[64] In Mughal India, it signified a person who held a portion of land registered in the *Khalsa* (revenue department) record as his *Zamindari* and who was held accountable for the fixed amount of revenue due to the state. Thus, they were revenue farmers similar to *Ijaredars*, in Nepal. During the Mughal rule in India, the *Zamindar* was one of the elite groups which was under heavy pressure and modified itself in order to meet contemporary policy requirements.[65] They constituted two major types primary and intermediary *Zamindars*.[66] The *Zamindary* system that prevailed in Nepal was more or less similar. According to some references, local revenue functionaries in some parts of the hill region were also called Jimindar. They acted as intermediaries in the villages. They

61. Yogi Narahari Nath, *Itihas Prakash Ma Sandhipatra Sangraha* (A Collection of Historical Documents in the Interpretation of History), Dang : Narahari Nath, 2022 V.S., p. 74.
— Banstola, f.n. 4 pp. 128-129.
62. Irfan Habib, *The Agraian System of Mughal India,* Bombay : Asia Publishing House, 1963, p. 140.
63. Akhtar, f.n. 1, p. 1.
64. Habib, f.n. 62, p. 184
65. S. Nurul Hassan, *Thoughts on Agrarian Relations in Mughal India, Delhi :* Moti Lall Benarasi Dass, 1993, pp. 32-42.
66. G.D. Sharma, Zamindars and Land Rights in South Gujarat During the 18th Century (Unpublished Seminar papers on Agrarian Relations in Medieval Deccan), Department of History, Poona, n.d., p. 1-17.

dealt with the tenancy and often managed credit supplies. All the intermediaries had the right to exact rent and taxes. Although they were given some privileges, their property rights were not recognized.[67] Their interests, though removable under pressure from the authorities, tended to become hereditary, and thereby transformed their revenue right into land rights.

The Community of Cultivators

> *"...the tenants must borrow seeds from the landlords, for this he pays 100 % interest, when he borrows a pair of bullock he must pay in rice and same when he borrows money from the landlord."*[69]

This observation in contemporary agrarian society clarifies the economic status of the cultivators.

The tenants furnished everything else for good production and good harvests. It was entirely their duty to cultivate the land and pay the landlords' share in whatever place he designated. Various available evidences suggest that the entire history of the Rana autocracy and its continued existence consisted robbing the toiling Nepalese peasantry. Thus, the reality of the contemporary agrarian system was, generally marked by the pauperization of the agrarian classes.[70] The peasant families were basically an economic unit, which produced adequate grain with which to pay rent and taxes and for their own subsistence. They were entirely limited by their economic needs. The tenants and other categories of cultivators were denied land rights. They were not able to transfer occupancy rights through sales and mortgages. Generally, the

67. Mahesh Chandra Regmi, *A Study of Nepali Economic History,* New Delhi : Manjus*ri* Publishing House, 1971, p. 92
68. Radha Kamal Mukharjee,'Land Tennur', in Edwin R.A. Sellingman (ed.)., *Encyclopaedia of The Social Sciences,* IX-X, New York : Mac Millian Company, 1957, pp. 110-112.
69. Wallinsky, f.n. 8, p. 318.
70. Ulyanovsky, f.n. 5, p. 68.

prevailing customs had safeguarded their right to cultivate. They could hold land as long as they kept the landowners and intermediaries satisfied, because the latter could evict tenants at will. The stronger position of the privileged classes, the worthless peasant economy, and widespread poverty made it easy for them to exploit the peasants as they desired. The peasants were compelled to cultivate land according to the will of the landowners. Generally, they cultivated land under the Adhiya system, so, they were not registered in revenue record as tenants. In this situation, they had to live at the mercy of the landlords. They had no significant land rights.

In the Karnali region too, the *Rajas* or *Jimindars* controlled vast areas of land. A major portion of the land was left uncultivated. On the other hand, the *Chuni* peasants played the role of an intermediary tenant. The *Jimidar*, *Chuni* and ordinary cultivators differed from each other and their land rights also varied to a great extent,[71] but the prevailing agrarian system encouraged agricultural tenancy in the far western hill region. The peasants in these areas enjoyed the customary practice of transferring their cultivation rights through sale or mortgage. This led to the remarkable development of a market for land transaction. It was a significant development on behalf of the cultivators, but on the whole, the cultivators were burdened by heavy and variable taxation, which precluded any saving.

The state's landlordism had played major role in creating intermediary practices in the land holding system, but similar system of Ryotwari in Bombay (Mumbai) and Madras (Chennai) which prevailed in certain parts of Nepal's Tarai did not recognize existence of intermediaries. In those areas, revenue settlements were made directly with the cultivators, as it was a common practice in India.[72] At the beginning of the Rana's rule, land which was kept uncultivated was allotted to peasants, but in the Eastern Tarai, Karnali region and some other parts of

71. Yogi Narahari Nath, f.n. 61, p. 379.
72. Romesh Chandra Dutt, *The Economic History of India,* New Delhi : Ministry of Broadcasting and Information, 1960, pp. 23-25.

the hill region, there were no intermediaries in *Raikar* land. The local revenue functionaries were involved in revenue matters on behalf of the regime. Their rights were confirmed by both customary and statutory measures. The intermediaries were very common in the hills in tenures other than the Raikar. In Raikar the local functionaries sometimes acted as the intermediaries, but it was possible only when the owner of the Raikar was not a local resident.

The intermediaries were one of the important groups in Nepal's land holding system. This group of people contributed to the separation of land ownership and cultivation. This had far reaching consequences in the agrarian system of the country. In fact, the unity of land ownership and use is positive in agrarian development. Therefore, the separation of these two is not desirable by any means.

The gross crop was divided into two halves- *Talsingboti* and *Mohiboti*. The *Talsingboti* was divided among the state, landowners and the intermediaries. The Land Act of 1957 regulated the traditional rent, but the Act also reduced rent to one half of the gross produce.[73] The indigenous landlordism and the traditional buttress of the regime expropriated the producer's right to his land.[74] The economy of Nepal from 1768 up to 1951 remained static, and was predominantly agrarian based. The peasants were those who produced capital to fulfill the interests of the landlords. Thus, the cultivators were blended by heavy and variable taxation. Long before the Rana regime,[75] Prithivi Narayan Shah, also created a system under which each local lord was provided with the opportunity to collect tax and they were held responsible for collecting tribute on their own or on behalf of the regime. The introduction of the Kut system in the twentieth century also provided an opportunity for the privileged classes to exploit the peasants according to their will. This kind of concealed robbery brought agriculture to an

---

73. 'Bhumi Sambandhi *Ain* 2014, f.n. 20, pp. 192-198.
74. Ulyanovsky, f.n. 5, p. 109.
75. Seddan *et al,* f.n. 40, p. 49.

unprecedented state of depletion in the twentieth century. The peasant community produced capital and paid rent. It was their duty to pay a share of produce to landowners, intermediaries and the local functionaries.[76] It is interesting to note that even at the height of power, the Mughal rule did not appear to have claimed greater rights than this.[77] So, the Nepalese peasantry was required to pay a large part of the agrarian produce in the form of rent and taxes. They even paid various customary levies regularly for nothing.

In order to study the agrarian system, the term peasant must be used meaningfully to describe a more or less homogenous and undifferentiated community of families characterized by small holdings, which were operated mainly by family labour.[78] Mahesh Chandra Regmi has identified three types of peasants in Nepal - firstly, peasants without protection, secondly, peasants having security against arbitrary eviction, but without property rights, and finally, peasants enjoying statutory security with limited (property) rights.[79] Rostislav Ulyanovsky, a well known Russian Indologist, has a different view of the typology of peasants in India. According to him, there were[80]

- Absolute perpetual tenants: higher castes and old feudal lords who enjoyed proprietary rights.
- Perpetual and intermediary tenants: Tenants who sub let land to others, and enjoyed certain land rights.
- Simple tenants: They could be thrown off the land only by the decision of the court, and
- Sub-tenants: They were the actual cultivators, without rights on the land they cultivated. This type of tenancy

76. 'Nepali's Land Reform', *Regmi Research Series,* Year 9, No, 10, Oct. 1977, p. 131.
77. Banstola, f.n. 4, pp. 109.
    Also see-*Report of the ....,* f.n. 34, p. 5.
78. Andre Beteille, *Studies In Agrarian Structure,* Delhi : Oxford University Press, 1974, p. 74.
79. Regmi, f.n. 18, pp. 505-525 and 759-763.
80. Ulyanovsky., f.n. 5, pp. 34-36 and 41-44.

was also very common in the later Rana period in Nepal and they were popularly known as tenants at will and share croppers.

The tenants in different forms of tenures held tenancy on a customary basis with legal agreements to define their position and rights. In British India, the rights and obligations of tenants with occupancy rights were defined by legislation, but the sharecroppers were not given any legal protection. There was insecurity of occupancy and widespread poverty among the sharecroppers. The political economists have agreed that such tenurial conditions are obstacle to economic development in many ways.[81] The landlords of Nepal exacted a large share in agrarian produce without incurring even a small part of its cost. It left a minimum amount for the cultivators without any margin for investment. It finally resulted in increasing trend of rural indebtedness and fostered the worst form of peasant economy. On the other hand, the accumulation of wealth did not lead to productive investment. The village landlords and moneylenders supplied agricultural credit to needy peasants. The accumulated capital in the hands of the landowners and moneylenders was not used in productive activities by any means.

The condition of the peasant cultivators before promulgation of the Land Reforms Act in 1964 was much worse in economic terms. The state took no account of poor peasants. The landlords and land holding intermediaries were favoured in one way or another. The ties between privileged and non-privileged classes were essentially economic rather than social or otherwise. In areas where *Birta, Jagir* and *Jimidari* existed, the intermediaries dealt with actual cultivators on behalf of the landlords. But in the central hill region where ownership of land was vested in the state (i.e. the *Raikar* tenure), the conditions of the peasants was not better in any sense in comparison to their counterparts in other tenures. Their conditions were not even better than those of tenants at-will,[82] and they lived under the worst

81. U.N.O., f.n. 15, p. 17.
82. Regmi, f.n. 17, p. 117.

conditions and in bare subsistence. Even the revolutionary act of 1964 left various grounds for eviction. The eviction of tenants was impossible in all tenures.

Wolf Ledijinsky has correctly described the condition of the peasantry before 1951 in the following words-

> *"... Where the land is scarce and competition for it intense, rental is two-third of the gross crop. This does not include other imposts including personal services and loans at usurious rates levied upon the tenants by landlords."*[83]

This situation tended to continue even after 1951. These were the overall conditions of the Nepalese peasantry. The peasants had no alternatives but to pay up to two-thirds of the gross product as rent. Furthermore, the landowners were entitled to exact other numerous taxes and levies. Ledjinsky further illustrates this as follows;

> *"...That some peasants do have a few Ropanis of land of their own, but this is seldom enough to provide them with any more than the customary meager living. Most farmers... had altogether too little land and were compelled to cultivate somebody else's land to meet their barest needs. Others had no land of their own whatsoever, and the peasant who spoke of his dream to die with a little land of his own voiced the thought of all the landless".*[84]

The status and conditions of Nepalese cultivators were exclusively based on customs and traditions rather than by statutes. It was a common practice among the landlords to appoint a new tenant. A cultivating tenant could easily be evicted at the will of the owners or land holding intermediaries if they

83. Wallinsky, f.n. 8, pp. 316-323.
84. *Ibid.*

so desired. The existing laws provided favourable situations for the landowners.[85] Although tenants were given customary protection against arbitrary eviction, the landowners had full authority to evict tenants if they refused to pay stipulated rents, taxes and levies. On the other hand, the introduction of the *Kut* system compelled cultivators to pay a fixed amount of rent. This system proved to be most unfavourable in comparison to sharecropping. Later on, the government attempted to bring about certain changes regulating the eviction of cultivating tenants, but it too, was not effectively done.

Gradually, the rights of cultivators began to emerge, they were given the right to transfer property under certain conditions. A good location of the plot, fertility, and the investment of labour and capital in the plot were factors under which cultivators were able to transfer their rights. During the latter half of the regime, tenants were given property rights on *Raikar* and *Jagir* lands. Thereafter, the tenants also sublet land for cultivation to bidders for higher profits. It finally contributed to the emergence of 'intermediary tenants' in the agrarian structure. In the central hill region, the local landowners obtained land from absentee landlords, but they did not cultivate it by themselves. They found other poor peasants to cultivate it. However, the Land Reforms Act of 1964 has eradicated the practice of such intermediate tenancy by those who held land belonging to absentee landlords but did not cultivate by themselves. In this case, the cultivators held land without any occupancy or property rights. In most cases, the local landowners acted as intermediaries for absentees. Under such conditions, the rights of actual cultivators were neither guaranteed nor secured.[86] On the other hand, the government officials also demanded supplies from peasants free of cost. Regmi has rightly observed that:

---

85. The Civil Code of 1910 V.S. and its subsequent amendments discussed and elaborated the rights and conditions of the priviledged classes.
86. Teodor Dhanin, *Peasants and Peasant Societies,* Middlesex : Penguin Books, 1975, pp. 103-114.

> *"In districts where military battalions were stationed, it was the duty of the local peasants to provide foodstuffs to feed them. Local military authorities paid for food supplies at prices lower than those current in the villages or sometimes without payment."*[87]

The peasants were compelled to provide foodstuffs to military. In both cases, they lost the amount. It was an additional burden for the poor peasants who were already under the unbearable burden of landowning elite. The peasants were in no condition to escape from such burden. The government policy in the latter Rana period was intended to grant certain rights to them, but the tradition did not provide a favourable basis for it. Therefore, the productive forces and production relations remained unchanged. Consequently, the production methods and technology remained as it had been in previous decades. But it is important to note that the peasant economy was ruined as the result of feudal oppression.[88] Even in contemporary society, although the Land Reform Act of 1964 has brought about significant changes in the agrarian system, prolonged sharecropping without written transactions represents more or less same characteristics.[89] Many of the features of the agrarian structure under the Ranas tended to continue. The *Kamaiya*, *Hali* and *Taluki* systems are still existent in many parts of the country as the legacy of feudal oppression. The *Kamaiya* (bonded labour) system is widely practiced in Dang, Bardiya, Banke, Kailali and Kanchanpur districts.[90] It is a system

87. Regmi, f.n. 17, p. 60
88. Ulyanovsky, f.n. 5, pp. 70-72.
89. *Bhumu Sambandhi Ain Thatha Niyamharu 2021 V.S.,* (Land Act and Land Laws 1964). Biratnagar : Nepali Sahitra Bhandar. 2023 V.S., pp. 3-18.
90. *A Study of Bonded Labour,* Kathmandu : Ministry of Labour and Social Welfare, n.d., pp. 11-15.
    Also see-*Nepalma Kamaiya Prathobhitra Bandha Majdoor* (Bonded Labour Within The Kamaiya System in Nepal), Kathmandu : INSEC, 2049 V.S., pp. 37-85.

under which cultivators remain merely tools of production rather than a force for socio-economic change. It has compelled thousands of poor peasants to remain in a state of perpetual slavery. In fact, they were tied in debt bondage for many generations. On the other hand, the Taluki system, which prevailed in the Far Western hill region also, contributed to the deterioration of the conditions of the peasant community.

The agrarian social structure during the Rana regime was almost same which prevailed before 1846 A.D. Therefore, the entire agricultural system was traditional. The system favored the privileged groups. The peasantry lived at the mercy of landlords. They produced capital primarily to pay rent and taxes to the landowners and ensure their cultivation rights. They cultivated land without any significant rights. Even though new legislation was promulgated, they could not find replacements at higher rental rates. The high rates of rent, the concentration of land rights in the privileged classes, growing rural indebtedness, and traditional types of credit supply became the dominant themes of contemporary rural economy. So, the peasants' conditions did not witness any significant changes throughout the Rana's rule. Only after 1964 were some changes initiated in the agrarian system. Although the Act of 1964 proved to be a landmark in the agrarian history of Nepal, it too, could not bring about complete reform. By the end of the Rana's rule in 1951, the active leadership of the peasantry on an ideological basis to bring about changes in the contemporary system and agrarian relations proved to be very effective. A large part of the Nepalese peasantry joined forces with the Marxist activists to demand desired reforms in agriculture and fulfill their dreams.

* * *

CHAPTER III

AGRARIAN PRODUCTION RELATIONS

Introduction:

Before proceeding to different aspects of the relationship between different groups in the agrarian social structure and the analysis of existing aspects of production relations on a theoretical basis, it is necessary to know about the term peasantry. Peasants are always the main force for capital production. The landlords stood at the middle of the relationship as a parasitic community who controlled the entire means of production. They were not required to play even a minor role in agrarian activities, but they remained dominant throughout the history of agriculture.

The analysis of different aspects of agrarian production relations in Nepal or elsewhere is, in fact, incomplete without considering the concept of peasantry as analyzed in various ideological writings. It helps to discuss the Nepali peasant community and labour relations using this paradigm.

Karl Marx and Fredrick Engels have stressed the political apathy of peasants, but the peasants are very essential factor in the population, production process, capital formation, and sometimes political power.[1] The Marxian view is very critical of peasants and has referred to them as a petit-bourgeoise class

---

1. Fredrick Engels, "The Peasant Question in France and Germany, in *Selected Works of Karl Marx and Fredrick Engels,* Vol. 3, Moscow : Progress Published, 1970, p.-74.

caricaturing them as a sack of potatoes that lacked interconnections, a common political identity and common organizations.[2] He even despised them as representing barbarism in the midst of civilization.[3] Despite such harsh criticism, the Marxist outlook on peasants is ambivalent. On the other hand, Engels held a balanced view of peasants along with a clearer understanding of the internal stratification and differentiation within a peasant society. He articulated his position on the role of newly emerging classes in the attainment revolutionary objectives . For him, the farm labourers were the most natural ally of the urban industrial proletariat rather than the tenant farmers or peasant proprietors.[4] He further analyzed the peasant community as an internally split, unorganized and politically impotent class unless mobilized by the organized working class.

Later, Lenin modified the Marxist view of peasants. The peasant force remained a single force in producing capital. It formed the great bulk of the revolutionary forces and revolutionary potential as well as provided power for capital formation.[5] Their potential is the primary reason that Plekhanov has described peasants not as a class but as a notion. It further indicates the potential of the peasantry as a force for either political or social change.

Lenin divided the peasant community into three groups - firstly poor peasants, secondly middle peasants and thirdly, the rich peasants.[6] The existing pressures of fierce competitions, impoverishment and inextricable indebtedness drove them to

2. Karl Marx and Fredrick Engels, *Selected Works,* Vol. 3, London : Lawrence and Wishart, 1968, pp. 174-178.
3. D.N. Dhanagare, *Peasant Movements in India 1920-1950,* New Delhi : Oxford University Press, 1944, p. 2.
4. Fredrick Engels, *The Peasant War in Germany,* London : Lawrence and Wishart, 1969, pp. 14-16.
5. Jean Chesnaux, *Peasant Revolts in China 1840-1849,* London : Thames and Hudson, 1973 pp. 121-160.
6. Vladimir I, Lenin, *Development of Capitalism in Russia-Collected Works III,* Moscow : Progress Publisher, 1964, pp. 71-80.

sell labour power on a regular basis to ensure their survival. This has been the distinguishing characteristic of Lenin's poor peasants. The conceptualized terminology of middle peasants was introduced for the first time in Lenin's writings. The middle peasants were distinguished from poor peasants and the peasant bourgeoisie. Their position was traditional and their income was somewhat lower than average and their position in the agrarian social structure was most unstable. They also used hired labour in agriculture but they supplied more workers. Their position was an extremely precarious one. The process of de-peasantization resulted from capitalist development in agriculture, swept away the middle peasant category and reinforced the extreme ones namely the peasant bourgeoisie and rural proletariat. Thus, Lenin and Mao Tse Tung categorized the rural society in five classes which were set in the structural hierarchy as follows -

Landlords, Rich Peasants, Middle peasants, Poor peasants and Rural proletariat.

On some occasions, however, other forms are also added on the basis of relations. The rich peasants are often described as the rural bourgeoisie. The area they cultivated exceeded the area that can not be worked with family labour alone. Therefore they hired the labourers required to cultivate it.[7]

Mao Tse Tung had his own views on peasants and the peasant economy. His model is more elaborate and is comprehensive enough to encompass pre-capitalist, quasi feudal landlord-tenant relations as well as capitalist relationship. His concept of middle class peasants refers to those who own land or own only a part of their land and rent all the remaining land. According to him, they derive their income wholly or partially from their own labour and as a rule they not exploit others. In many cases, the mid level peasants were exploited by others during the payment of rent and interest on loans. Although, in exceptional cases, the middle class peasants exploited others,

7. Atiur Rahman, *Peasant and Classes : A study of Differentiation in Bangladesh,* Delhi : Oxford University Press, 1986, pp. XX.

it was not considered to be their main source of income. In Mao's assessment, the middle peasants or the owner peasants had typical petite-bourgeoisie predilections and were afraid of revolution, whereas the poor peasants were more revolutionary than the middle peasants.[8]

The peasant discontent and protest against the prevailing system frequently centered upon correcting defective agrarian relations and egalitarian social order rather than the hierarchical present. It intended to create a golden age of justice and equality through the establishment of a new order on earth.[9] In fact, such a desire animated revolutionary activities in many countries, including Nepal in the twentieth century and so forth. History has proved that such higher expectations of changes within the existing structure even mobilized the peasant community to the point of staging typical bloody rebellions. The peasant leaders are the most celebrated personalities in almost every peasant community. They are the champions of their people. They exact revenge or redress wrongs; they claim land for the landless.[10] The peasant discontent prevalent in agriculture during the Rana regime was not always limited to professional interests. it was not always aimed at the revolutionary restructuring of the society in favour of the peasant cultivators. Most often they were guided by ideology or non-professional factors. The observation of Hobsbawm is appropriate to cite here-

> *"It protests not against the fact that peasants are poor and oppressed but against the fact that they are sometimes excessively poor and oppressed. Bandit heroes are not expected to*

---

8. Mao-tse Tung, *Selected Works* Vol. 1, Peking : Foreign Language Press, 1967 pp. 15-20.
9. Eric Wolf, *Peasants,* New Jersey, Printice Hall Inc., 1966 p. 106.
10. *Ibid,* p. 107.
    Also See-Ram Bahadur Jyapu, *Nepalma Kisan Andolan Ko Ek Jhalak* (An Outline of Peasant Movement In Nepal), Kathmandu : Yuba Sahitya Gosthi, n.d., pp. 13-16/39-41.

> *make a world of equality. They prove that sometimes oppression can be turned upside down. Beyond that the bandit hero is merely a dream of how wonderful it would be if times were always good".*[11]

Even in Nepal, the discontent among the peasantry right at the end of the Ranas' rule was mostly led by the communists for their own ideological expansion. This dialectic was at work more powerfully even after 1960 under the totalitarian Panchayat rule. The peasants supported the communists because the latter talked about emancipation and transformation to modernity, which made the peasant community curious to prick up their ears and listen to land reforms. On the other hand, they also provided capable leadership and a force of professional revolutionaries whose function was to provide an ideological strategy. They led peasants to express their dissatisfaction. In fact, those leaders were able to lead successful movements and the prolonged social disorder beyond repair.[12] The peasant discontent and existing agrarian relations which weighed heavily upon the peasantry finally motivated them to participate in such activities, but such activities, in Nepal's case, are not always aimed at improving conditions for the peasantry. For instance, *Chhintang* the uprising in Dhankuta, Eastern Nepal and *Piskar* in Sindhupalchok district in the central hills fall within this category.[13] The peasant force itself aimed at the subjugation and transformation of the peasant community into a new kind of social grouping.[14] The existing socio-economic conditions, power and domination of the privileged classes, lack of educational opportunities, inability to analyze their own

---

11. E.J. Hobsbawn, *Primitive Rebels Studies in Archaic Forms of Social Movement in the Nineteenth and Twentieth centuries,* Manchester : Manchester University Press, 1959, pp. 24-25.
12. Wolf, f.n. 9, p. 108.
13. Evaluation of Chhintang Massacre, *Barga Sangharsha,* No. 15, Shrawan 2045, pp. 67-76.
14. Wolf, f.n. 9, pp. 108-110.

conditions, the remnants of medieval feudalism etc. made them weakest within the social structure. Under these conditions, peasants were not organized by themselves. For many centuries they expected to bring about a system of transcendental justice, a complete revolutionary change, and social equality. This common myth among the peasantry united them to raise their voices against usury and malpractice and was ultimately intended to introduce changes in the agrarian structure and relationship. But one should be aware of the fact that peasant rebellions or peasant coalitions are unstable and shifting alliances of antagonistic and autonomous units were driven only temporarily and by a millennial dream.[15] Everywhere, the peasants were suppressed and exploited. Even the state protected the economic interests of the gentry against the interests of the cultivating peasants. The state did not pay attention to the latter's welfare. Consequently, sometimes peasant rebellions were suppressed. The short term individual peasant interests took precedence over any long term ends. On the other hand, peasant subsistence, every day concerns, state policy, privileged classes in agrarian relations etc. all compelled them to halt on the middle of the way and pushed them back to daily life. So, the peasants who were united for one dream quickly relapsed into quiescence and remained passive. Hence, it is hypothesized that if peasant unity remains intact or does not relapse, the accumulated discontent and dissatisfaction could emerge as a remarkable force to bring about changes. The discontent created so far by existing injustice and traditional agrarian relations played a vital role in conflicts between the classes of landlords, tenants, and cultivators. The unlimited power of the landowners, the desperate economic conditions of the peasant community, and traditional agrarian practices remained vital in the agrarian production relations of that time.

The Conceptual Basis of Relations

Since the remote past, agrarian society has been organized

15. *Ibid.*

on the basis of the landlord tenant relationship in places where agriculture remained a primary economic activity. The term 'agrarian and production relations' denotes a bipolar relationship between the parties involved in agriculture with specific rights and duties. This relationship is essentially based on economic terms rather than any other social connotations. The agrarian relationship is the relationship between the state, landlords, intermediaries, local revenue farmers, village functionaries, tenants, the actual cultivators and labourers. As a matter of fact, the interests, rights and duties of all such agrarian groups were related to a particular piece of land which they shared with each other. The study of agrarian relations within this boundary involves the relationship between the state and landlords, the state and the peasants, landowners and the intermediaries, intermediaries and cultivators, landlords and tenants and landowners and the agraristic serfs or cultivators and labourers.[16] This relationship further represents land as a systemic unity.[17]

The ways and processes of sharing rights and claims in the means of production and the production itself between the concerned agrarian groups is a core aspect of the agrarian relationship. In this process, the landlords or other privileged classes always remained dominant in the relationships. Agrarian relations are a special case of dyadic ties involving a largely instrumental friendship in which an individual from the higher strata in the society uses his own strength, influences and resources to provide protection for a person from the lower strata who, for his part, reciprocates by offering general support

16. K.S..Shivanna, The Agrarian Relations With Special Reference to Revenue Terms As Reflected In Kannada Inscriptions During The 17th & 18th Centuries', (Unpublished seminar paper on Agrarian Relations In Maharastra), Poona : Department of History University of Poona, 1985, P-1.
17. Brian J. Murton, 'Land and Class : Cultural, Social and Biophysical Integration in Interior Tamil Nadu in the Late 18th Century', In Robert Eric Frykenberg (ed.), *Land Tenure and Peasants In Sourth Asia,* New Delhi : Manohar Publications, 1972, pp. 81-82.

and assistance, including personal services to the patron.[18] The ways and stages, in which how peasants and landowners are related to each other and factors that govern their relationship in any socio-economic ties are discussed in the agrarian relations of a particular community, society or country.

In almost all of customary tenures, the owners of large size holdings enjoyed various privileges. It made them the renting class in the country. It has been a common phenomenon in the capitalist form of economy. The size of holdings and conditions under which it is conducted are correlated to each other. Where holdings are small, cultivation through tenants would hardly be worthwhile unless the owners have an alternative source of income. The work force within the household or exchanged labour were used to cultivate land. The production relations and sharing of the gross product are important factors to analyze both the agrarian structure and agrarian relations. Production was socially organized to the extent that it involved relations between persons having more or less specific rights, duties and other obligations with regard to each other. Production relations tend to create divisions as well as bonds between the classes.[19]

The agrarian production relationship is an economic relationship among the people in the agrarian society which influences the factors concerning production or resources in agriculture as well as the pattern of distribution of its yield. In the nineteenth century, the government of India also referred to agrarian relations as consisting of the relative rights, interests and privileges of various classes in the agricultural community, owning, occupying or cultivating the land and sharing its produce, proceeding upwards from the persons who till the land to the government itself.[20] The agricultural production activities

18. H. Lakshminarayan and S.S. Tyagi, *Changes In Agrarian Structure In India,* New Delhi : Agricole Publishing Company, 1982, p. 12.
19. Andre Beteille, *Class, Caste and Power Changing Pattern of Straification in a Tanjore Vilalge,* Berkeley : University of California Press, 1965, pp. 110-111.
20. Sulekh Chandra Gupta, *Agrarian Relations and British Rule in India,* Bombay : Asia Publishing House, 1963, p.-1.

were carried out by the members of the agricultural community, particularly the peasant cultivators, within the framework of the economic relations. The growth, development or decay of agriculture had been influenced in an important manner by the nature of the rights, duties and privileges of different classes in the agrarian hierarchy.[21] The agrarian relationship is essentially an economic relationship that ignored all kinds of social ties. The social or other ties remained less important than the economic relationship. The basic trends in agrarian relations in South Asia in the nineteenth and twentieth centuries reflected ways of accommodating interests from the peasants to the biggest landlords. The relationship between landlord and tenants, and in general terms, the leaser and the leasee always loomed large in terms of property laws since the early days of civilization. Not only land and dwellings, but also buildings and immaterial things have been leased. It further developed various interests, rights and relationships through the particular object which had been leased so far. The landowners, land holding intermediaries, tenants, and the cultivating contractual parties all had vested interests in the land. The contractual relations focused on special ties between the parties in the contract. The relations between landlords and tenants, landowners and the land holding intermediaries, landholders and cultivating peasants or sub-tenants existed side by side. All such relations tended to become ambivalent. The structure of these relationships reflected the ways in which numerous interests were accommodated on a scale which reaches from the tiller of the soil to the highest authority of the state. The status of the landlords and tenants varied according to the specific place they held in the structure of the agrarian society.[23] Lenin also held the view -

21. *Ibid.*
22. A.C. Jacobs, 'Landlord and Tnant', In Edwin R.A. Selligmann, (ed.), *Encyclopaedia of Social Science* Vol. 9, New York: Mac Millian Co, 1957, 143-147.
23. Dietmar Rothermund, 'Government, Landlords and Tenants in India 1857-1900', Reprint from-*The Indian Economic and History Journal* Vol. VI, No. 4. Dec 1969, Heidelberg : South Asia Institute of University of Heidelberge, pp. 351-352.

> *"...the pressure of medieval relations and systems of land ownership, bondage and tyranny, the more strongly do capitalist relationship develop within the peasant farming."*[24]

As he suggested, the relations that were influenced by the medieval pattern of ties and land holding, the land management system and all other socio-economic phenomenon in the present context system tended to create a capitalist relationship. That kind of relationship was prevalent both in colonial India and in Nepal at that time. The involved parties in agrarian relations constituted the economic classes. It has been a general phenomenon that the claim of the privileged classes to the surplus product grew to excess. Sometimes, it created dissatisfaction and precipitated an outburst of peasant movements. The dissatisfaction of the peasantry exploded everywhere where that the agricultural system provided such a base. For instance, dissatisfaction also broke out in the permanently settled *Zamindari* in Bengal (1793) in an organized form in 1859, 1885 and 1928. Peasant movements in Nepal started in 1951 when there was an adequate base for it. Such a situation always caused to bitterness in agrarian relations. The politically tight regime in Nepal did not witness any organized resentment against the ruthless exploitation of peasants until the end of the Rana regime. There was no attempt from the people's side to bring about changes in the existing form of agrarian relations during the Rana regime because the aristocracy had a tight grip on its population. In fact, the relationship was imposed from above. Therefore, it maintained the status quo throughout the regime. Within the framework of such relations, the usurious revenue farmers, landowners, the intermediaries, and the village moneylenders all intended to exploit the peasantry and exact benefit from the traditional relationship.

Agrarian relations could be studied in terms of various socio-

24. Ian Roxborough, *Theories of Underdevelopment,* London : MacMillian Co, 1979, pp. 2-5

economic variables. The land-rent composition, rural indebtedness, credit supply, tenancy, occupancy right and rights and privileges of landlords and other privileged groups are widely accepted variables to study patterns of agrarian relations. In the same way, the customary practices also play an important role in it. Therefore, the traditional factors which influenced the patterns of agrarian relations should not be ignored while dealing with agrarian relations. This factor contributed in shaping agrarian relationship in the traditional societies which is, often found to be uniform.[25] It revealed the exact nature of relations in the feudal system. Basically, the relationship between landlords and tenants is the impetus in agrarian studies. Because the landlord's status is superior to that of the tenants, they could hardly avoid existing tenurial conditions and relieve the pressure.[26] In such a situation, cases of resistance against the landlords by the oppressed cultivators would be very few. If there were any, it was not hard to suppress them. In fact, the control of the regime over its subjects had a significant impact in determining agrarian relations. In connection with such relations, no satisfactory protection was provided to cultivators, both in India and Nepal. This type of situation is usually, aggravated by the extreme difficulty of finding a proper basis of legislation between the classes and the masses.[27]

The primary factor, which determines the relationship is tenancy. Tenancy in itself, obviously, is not bad where tenants enjoy a reasonable degree of security and stability and rent is not exorbitant.[28] The cultivators in Nepal were not given any substantial land rights. In fact, the Rana period witnessed the worst form of tenancies.

---

25. Ian Roxborough, *Theories of Underdevelopment,* London :MacMillian Co, 1979, pp. 2-5
26. Akria Takahasi, *Land and People in Central Luzon,* Honolulu : East West Center 1969, p. -74
27. Romesh Chadra Dutt, *The Economic History of India,* New Delhi : Ministry of Information and Broadcasting, 1960, p. -197.
28. V. Webster Johnson and Releigh Barlowe, *Land Problems and Policies,* New York : Mac Graw Hill Book Co., 1954, pp. 389-391.

The production relationship and process are important variables with which to study agriculture. They involve relations between persons having more or less specific rights, duties or obligations with regard to one another. The production relations tend to create divisions as well as bonds between the classes. The separation of ownership and cultivation of the land has been well accepted land practice in Nepal since long ago. Having an unequal pattern of land ownership, it displays four basic relations, specially the relations between the owners and cultivators, landholders and cultivators, leasers, and sharecroppers, and cultivators and labourers.[30] These basic relations created various rights and duties with respect to one another. The production relations in Nepal during the Rana regime entailed the following, which is clearly shown in the chart below (next page).

Production Relations Between Agrarian Groups :

The pattern of agrarian and production relations in Nepal was most traditional in nature during both the Shah and the Rana regimes. It tended to continue without basic changes even after the revolution of 1951. Until 1964, there was hardly any legal promulgation to bring about complete changes in the existing pattern of agrarian behaviour. Basically, the relationship between different agrarian groups involved directly or indirectly with the land is dealt with here. But it is a broader term that covers all other aspects, such as the role of agrarian groups in agricultural production, the division of product of the soil, the roles and obligations to be fulfilled during production activities, and their impacts on peasant economy.

The existing agrarian social structure in the country determined most of the factors in such relations. Therefore, the production relationship has always been a relative matter in agriculture, and is interrelated with all the groups in agriculture.

---

30. G.P. Mishra, *Some Aspects of Change in Agrarian Relations,* (Institute of Socio-economic Change monograph-4), New Delhi : Sterling Publisher, 1977, p.-1.

The pattern of relationships covers all the influencing situations and factors. Therefore, it is necessary to understand it before proceeding to analyze it. The diagram (appendix- 2 and 3) explains the contemporary production relations.

This diagram clarifies the chain of agrarian groups involved in agriculture and their interrelationships. Thus, the production relations itself fell against the non-privileged classes. Production activities were initiated by the cultivators themselves. But the structure reflects the way in which numerous interests were accommodated.[31] The agrarian system within this kind of framework represents semi-feudalism. There were no any duties legally prescribed for upper class elite. The elementary form of commodity production, exaction of surpluses and economic condition of cultivators also created the network of traditional relationship.[32] Therefore, in a rural society the traditional type of production process and production relations and channelization of entire produce of the soil are more or less tied with different nature of socio-economic relationship. At the same time, the economic condition of tenant cultivators also led to influence the agrarian and production relations. The production relations and production process prevalent on the eve of 1846 remained unchanged until the 1950s. It further contributed to the development of a powerful capitalist relations.

The study of agrarian relationships in traditional and pre-industrial society is marked by inequality. The lower strata was usually imposed upon, with the burden of having to fulfil the landowning groups' interests. The capital they produced was exacted by the privileged classes through the collection of revenue, rent, taxes, customary levies and interest on loans. This relationship had to change for the economic betterment of the cultivating classes. The payment of rent and taxes has been important process in agrarian relations. The Nepalese landowning elite enjoyed various privileges and exacted

---

31. Rothermund, f.n, 23, p.-353.
32. Sohan Ram Yadav, *Nepal Feudalism and Rural Formation,* New Delhi : Cosmo Publicatons, 1984, p-19.

exorbitant rates of rent and taxes. Generally, in the traditional societies, the gross produce was channeled to various agrarian groups. But usually, the government's share was very low, and was paid by the landowners registered in revenue cadasters as *Mohi* or tenants. The owners of *Birta* and *Jagir* tenures, religious propensities, and others shared a high proportion of the agricultural products. In addition to this, these were tax free holdings; they were not required to pay revenue to the government.

The evolution of land laws and other related regulations helped in shaping agrarian relations and sometimes to correct defective relationships. The unequal pattern of relationships could be narrowed through such measures. On the other hand, some of the factors, including socio-economic status, possession of property etc. are also effective in determining and shaping agrarian relations and production. Regarding the relations which were related to agricultural production, the caste background of the involved parties, educational achievement and property all played a vital role. In fact, the legal enactment regulating land and related matters have started to change the nature of agrarian relations in many countries. In traditional societies, the state always attempted to maintain a traditional pattern of agrarian relations. This was because the ruling elite were closely associated with the landed aristocracy, who wanted to preserve their rights, interests and privileges. without performing any kind of role in the production process.

All relationships between land owners and cultivators remain very important for the entire production processes. The traditional type of agrarian relations always tended to favour the landowning elite. The agrarian relations under the Rana regime in Nepal represented the tacit acceptance of the system that prevailed during the previous regime. The former regime favoured the continuity of old institutions related to agrarian relations. The large scale land owners were either from the royalty, nobility or bureaucracy, so, they aimed to serve the interests of the ruling families, their relatives, and the nobility. Such interests were essentially political and economic. The principal concern of the Rana regime was to earn as much as possible. Although the system in Nepal was affected very little by the impact of colonial India at this time in history, the basic trends of agrarian relations, particularly the sharing of the gross crop and the privileged status of the elite were very similar. Some of the reflections of *Manusmriti* and Kautiliya's *Arthashastra* have influenced agrarian relationships and their domination by the elite throughout the period. There were also some indigenous institutions which reflected types or sub-types of agrarian relations. Those aspects include the *Parma* and *Mankajya* (both terms denotes to the exchange of labour). Those institutions were related to the traditional behaviour of the society.

An approach to the analysis of agrarian production relations requires the consideration of some of its factors. These relations were channeled i.e. one channel and multi channel relations, which denote the relationship within one layer between various layers in the hierarchy of the groups. The relationship between agrarian parties in tenures such as the *Raikar, Birta, Jagir, Guthi* and *Kipat* have certain variations. Differences are found in the sharing of products, the nature of land holding, occupancy and proprietary rights, and tenancy. Except in the *Raikar* tenure, the landowners in all the other tenures were virtual proprietors of the land. The cultivators cultivated land with or without occupancy rights. In all of these situations, the nature of the relationship was mostly determined by the payment of rent, taxes, customary levies and by fulfilling other obligations. Therefore, the basic component of the relationship was the fulfillment of duties and obligations. The normal result was that the cultivators were hindered by heavy and variable taxation which precluded any saving. This phenomenon has been a historical fact in all such societies.[33] The revenue and other taxes were tightly imposed on the cultivating classes. The rate of rent prevalent in Nepal was excessively high, ranging from one half to two thirds of the gross product until 1957, when the

33. Dutt, f.n. 27, p.-XV.

Land Act fixed rent at one half of the gross product. In this way, the existing pattern of relations itself was responsible for abysmal conditions of the peasantry. The existing land laws fixed rent and taxes in *Raikar*, but the customary rent system that prevailed for centuries in tenures other than the *Raikar* was never considered to be against the law. In fact, the landowners in the *Birta, Jagir, Rakam, Guthi* and the land holding intermediaries were authorized to settle rent according to existing customary practices. They rented land for cultivation under their own terms. They usually made rent settlements with the intermediaries, and then the later made settlements with the agent-tenants, tenants, sub-tenants or cultivators of any category. This rent system settlement had a greater impact in setting agrarian relations, but it did not favour better conditions for the peasantry.

Land ownership was concentrated in a low percentage of the population. The ruling families, aristocracy and nobility controlled a considerable area of land, thereby controlling the entire rural population. They were able to keep the ordinary population within their grip through land ownership. Almost all of the cultivators held land at the mercy of the landowners and the intermediaries. There were numerous burdens that gave cultivators no chance to avoid their immediate consequences and think beyond a subsistence life style. The lack of peasants' rights on the land had created such a situation.

Traditional agrarian relations in Nepal were primarily determined by the cultivation of land and payment of rent, so, the relationship was essentially based on economic terms more rather than any other social factor. Thus, economy had been the fundamental factor which to determine agrarian relations in Nepal. In fact, such a relation in traditional agrarian society is guided by terms and conditions of cultivation, the kind and procedure of rent and tax payment and socio-economic ties. The economic factor always remained dominant throughout the period in the relations between agrarian groups.

The landowning community placed the highest priority on collecting rent and associated customary levies. In this situation, the existing law and royal verdicts always favoured the rent receiving classes. The high rate of rent and its collection system had a profound impact in the relationship between landlords & tenants, landlords & intermediaries, intermediaries & cultivating tenants, and tenants & sharecropping sub-tenants. The absence of cultivators' land rights caused further deterioration of the peasant economy. Their financial ability also played a vital role in agrarian relations. The cultivators in all tenures were required to pay rent and taxes from the month of *Mangshir* to *Jestha* otherwise they would be evicted by landowners or the local *Mukhiya* and *Jimmawals*. The *Talukdars, Mukhiyas* and *Jimmawals* were fully responsible for rent payment in *Jagir* tenures. Although tenants were denied payment for rent, they had to reimburse rent to the *Jagirdars*, or they could not collect it for any other reasons. They were also required to pay a share to the government. They would be dismissed from their jobs as Talukdars if they failed to do so. The Sanads also mentioned rent collection on Jagera land in detail. The *Jagera* land as such was under state ownership and was kept as surplus land to grant to the *Jagirdars*. In 1959 V.S.. (1902 A.D.) the Prime Minister issued a *Rukka* regarding *Jagera* cultivation and revenue collection. It ordered the *Sirdars*, *Kharidars* and *Mukhiyas* (the civil servants) to act accordingly-

— Collect rent annually from Jagera land and retain 10% of total collection as *Khangi*. The arrears of *Jimmawals* in *Jagera* land should be collected from *Marga* to *Jestha* and prepare a receipt in the name of *Jimmawals*.

— The arrears should not extend beyond three years and collection, and exemption, if necessary, should be made within three years.

— The revenue must be collected from cultivators from *Marga* to *Jestha* and to issue necessary receipts in the name of the tenants. The Talukdars were required to remit the dues (collected amount) from *Mangsir* to *Jestha* in the *Bakyauta Tahasil Adda* and obtain the receipt. If the tenants refused to pay, they were supposed to be evicted according to the law. The same rule was applicable to the *Talukdars*.

— If *Jimmawals* reported the on non-payment of rent by tenants, the *Adda* should proceed to auction the land. But if anyone agreed to pay arrears and request to obtain land, the *Jimmawals* could evict the former tenant and appoint a new one.

— If a *Jimmawal* was to be dismissed due to the inability to collect rent from the tenants and remit arrears, an individual was to be appointed as the *Jimmawal* by tenants as desired.

— In case a tenant is evicted, all arrears should be paid by the new tenant. If the latter did not pay it, any individual who agreed to pay would be appointed as a tenant to cultivate land.

— In *Thek-Ijara* (contractual) settlement of Jagera land, the revenue should be increased and collected in two installments. If it is not settled accordingly, revenue should be collected on the basis of *Amanat* system.

— In case of natural calamities, revenue exemption would be granted to tenants on the basis of existing rules and

— The tenants were exempted form rent if arrears accumulated for a certain number of years. The years were fixed as 2 years for grandfather's arrears, 10 years for fathers and 20 years for current arrears.[34]

Those village functionaries were granted the power to deal with tenants and sharecroppers in revenue matters in the *Raikar* tenure. In other tenures, the land holding intermediaries dealt with the cultivators. There was a similar practice in the *Birta* & *Jagir* tenures. Tenants of all kinds had to contact village functionaries about any kind of land problem. They had no direct relationship with the state. In the western hill region, the landlords, *Talukdars* or *Mukhiya* and *Jimmawals* were officially authorized to collect rent from cultivators of *Jagera* land, but

34. 'Order regarding collection of revenue in Jagera land-1959 V.S.:' Poka no. 159, Record Section of the Department of Revenue.

in specific cases, the tenants of *Jagera* land were also exempted from rent payment. The *Talukdars, Jimmawals* and *Mukhiyas* were to be punished if they could not remit rent on behalf of the New Bakyauta Tahasil Adda in their areas. The nature of the punishment was to be decided by the premier. If they did not remit rent they were to be detained by the district court. In that case, the district administration had to provide food to such detainees.[35] This factor had become a dominant theme in the relationship between them. Thus, they began to take tougher measures against the tenants during rent and tax collection to avoid displeasing the rulers. This situation also led to the deterioration of the peasants' conditions. The tenants who failed to make rent payments were liable for imprisonment. The people who employed tenants were required to provide food. An order to Dailekh Gaunda mentioned that there were individuals who did not pay taxes, and such dues were not to be exempted according to existing laws. Such dues occurred because of -

— misplacement of tax payment receipts
— natural calamities
— defaulting
— poverty of cultivators whose income totaled less than the amount of taxes and
— Intentional refusal to pay taxes on the part of peasants.

In such cases, the government could not collect taxes without taking tough measures or detention. In case of detention, there was the problem of providing them with food. It was the moral duty of the regime to provide them with food, but it was not permitted by the Ain. So, the regime usually avoided such detentions.[36] The *Amali, Thani, Jimmawal* and other local functionaries were authorized to evict Raikar tenants

35. 'Order regarding imprisonment of tenants and provide food Ashwin 1959 V.S.:', Poka no. 159, S. No. 903, Record Section of the Department of Revnue.
36. 'On payment of rent 1959 V.S.:', Poka no. 159, S. no. 870, Record Section Department of Revenue.

in accordance with the law. But in other tenures, the landowners were authorized to evict tenants and cultivate land by themselves. The cultivating tenants of Rakam land such as *Hulak, Byang, Bosi, Ghasi, Bala, Golya* and *Barudhana Rakams* could refuse to cultivate. Under such conditions, the *Mukhiya, Dware* and *Pradhans* of *Rakam* tenures had to release them after completing a formal written procedure. Those tenants had no rights to claim land, otherwise they would be fined Rs. 2.50. The *Rakam Naikes* (leaders) could appoint other tenants for cultivation.[37] On *Birta* lands, the *Birtawala* had the right to choose his tenants and could rent land to higher bidders, but they could not evict tenants from *Sripanchami* to *Dashain* in the hills and *Sithinakha* to *Dashain* in the Kathmandu valley. It was probably because the cultivating season fell with in this period. In *Khangi* land, it was even necessary to rent land for higher bidders. The existing *Ain* allowed land rental to higher bidders, but the *Ain*, on the other hand, stated that contracts which had already been concluded were not to be canceled. If anyone evicted cultivating tenants for the purposes of higher bidding, it was considered illegal. However, the *Ain* did not elaborate on this situation. Therefore, the highest bidder had right to obtain *Jagir- Khangi* land even if it had been contracted already. It became a common practice. If the authorized person did not permit the latter, the regime threatened him to take action to violate the rule.[38] Thus, in the privileged tenures, the tenants were not protected and were evicted at the will of the owners or intermediaries. The time restriction had been an ordinary form of security against arbitrary eviction. On *Raikar* land or homestead sites, the tenants were assured of security until they paid rent and taxes, but it was an offense to let land remain uncultivated. If land was not cultivated, a tenant might be evicted

37. *Sri Panch Surendra Ko Pala Ma Baneko Muluki Ain,* Kathmandu : Ministry of Law and Justice, 2022 V.S., pp. 38-46.
The various *Rokams* include - *Silautey, Saliana, Kothabosi, Karmi, Atasbaji, Lamapathi* etc.
38. 'On Renting land to higher bidder - 1924 V.S...., Poka No. 12, Record Section of the Department of Revenue.

and another appoint was to be made. The tenants of *Birta, Guthi, Rakam, Jafati Jagga, Jagir* and *Jagera* land were legally authorized to till until they paid rent and taxes such as *Chardamtheki, Serma, Sauneyfagu*, etc. There was a statutory settlement that a tenant should not be evicted as long as he paid rent and taxes regularly.[39] It was the system that kept relations in tact in Raikar. They had to pay such a high rate of rent and taxes to individual proprietors in spite of crop failure in order to continue cultivation as the tenant. Even after the Land Reform Act of 1964 was promulgated, the relations between landlords and tenants remained very similar even though it brought changes in the basic nature of agrarian relations. At present too, the payment of rent is compulsory even at the crop failure. Even the owners have the right to claim it. During the Rana regime, the tenants requested exemption from rent in the event of crop failure. But crops destroyed due to famine, flood, fire or the encroachment of wild animals was subjected to exemption or reassessment. Thus, rent was to be fixed according to productivity.[40] Although there was a statutory settlement concerning rent reduction or exemption, the village functionaries and landowners seldom gave concessions for rent. They usually compelled and forced cultivators to pay rent. Sometimes, the latter could not tolerate the pressure and fled from the village to petition the premier against the usurious Zamindars. The rigidity and strictness of Zamindars and other intermediaries proved to be a burden to the toiling peasantry. The usurious Zamindars were tough against the peasant cultivators. In 1931 V.S.. (1874 A.D.), a petition was registered by a poor suppressed peasant against the usurers. It reflects the entire situation of Nepalese agriculture which prevailed during the Rana regime. The petition mentioned—

39. 'On eviction of Tenants' Poka No. 36, Record Section of the Department of Revenue.
40. *Shri Panch Surendra....*, f.n. no. 37, p. 46

"The numbari land of the 1925 V.S.. survey registered in my name was destroyed by flood in 1927 V.S.. The Amal (representatives) of Sadar Adalat, Amini, Kathmahal, and Mal Adda (Revenue Office), and Chaudhuri, Kanugoye, Patuwari and others inspected and approved it. The Mal Adda tax arrear was exempted by the Mal Adda and informed that the Khangi (unirrigated dry land assigned as Jagir) land Kut will be exempted by the jimidar. The Mal did not accept the request. But Nanda Raya, the Jimidar of the Mauja (area) was to remit Rs 1500 as Pota tax arrears for the years 1927 V.S.. to 1931 V.S (1870-1874 A.D.). He pressured me and compelled me to pay. So, I fled from the village and came to petition Your Highness. He has no right to claim on it because the Mal has already exempted taxes in adjoining holding."

The premier issued a Sanad on the issue which is very important in the contemporary agrarian relations. The premier ordered the district administrator to make the Jimidar present and inform him about the Rukka (order). If he agreed, the arear would be exempted according to the existing rules and customs that prevailed in the area. If the jimidar refused, the case was to be proceed and decided exactly on the basis of evidence.[41] It was a common practice that the dominant status of landlords and other privileged classes played a vital role in appropriating their share of the gross crop.

The relationship between landlords and tenants in terms of rent payment was mostly controlled by the landlords and intermediaries. They had to deliver rent as the landowners' wishes, but the owners had no right to claim a type of rent that differed from the agreement reached at the time of the contract

41. 'On claim for exemption of rent and complaint against usurious Zamindars Poka No. 36, Record Section of the Revenue Department.

for cultivation. The cultivators deserved right to pay as determined in the contract. Therefore, a landowner or an intermediary could not demand rice if he had already agreed to accept rent in cash,[42] but the tenants were required to pay within the prescribed time. The tenants who did not pay rent within the prescribed time schedule were liable for eviction or to be punished accordingly. The punishment was either a cash penalty or imprisonment according to the amount to be paid.[43] The *Jimmawals* and *Mukhiyas* were given the right to evict defaulting tenants, but under some conditions, rent exemption was permitted. In fact, the destruction of grain by fire or natural calamity within the prescribed period grounds for exemption. But unpleasant destruction of crop beyond the prescribed time did not provide any opportunity for exemption. Therefore, the peasants were ordered to pay within the fixed time period. There were many cases of this nature that were reported. Even the *Patuwari* and other rich people in the area manipulated existing laws and customary practices to benefit themselves. So, the tenants or peasant cultivators were exploited through different means. Sometimes, the *Patuwaris* in the Tarai did not take the *thekka* amount from the tenant as mentioned in the contract (*Sapurtanamah*). In one case, the owner of *numbari* land refused to accept rent from the cultivators. The *Patuwari* also acted against the common practice of registering land in the name of the contracting cultivator. The owner refused to accept the *thekka* amount to obtain rice if the harvest was good. In fact, the owners in the Tarai were required to accept the thekka amount if it was decided to do so.[44]

The *Dware, Pradhan, Mohinaike, Dhokrey, Praja, Mijhar, Mukhiya* (landholding intermediaries and local revenue functionaries)and *Mohi* (tenants) were also ordered to cultivate

42. 'Order on the case of types of payment 1930 V.S..., Poka 36, S. No. 217, D. No. 27, Record Section of the Revenue Department.
43. '*Sri panch Surendra ko....*, f.n. 37, pp. 48-50
44. 'Order regarding payment of rent on time and denial of tax exemption 1959 V.S....,' Poka No. Record Section, Department of Revenue.

the *Khangi* land of various *Jagirdars.* The cultivators were required to cultivate land but they were not allowed to leave land uncultivated. Even if there was no cultivation, the tenants were required to pay rent and to build irrigation facilities. If any one did not participate in it and left land uncultivated, he was required to pay rent at the same price as adjoining holdings and was also subject to punishment. The *Amali* and *Mohinaikye* were also made responsible for any failure to cultivate.[45]

Although the ultimate proprietor of all *Khangi* and *Jagir* land was the state, the *Jagirdars* enjoyed all possible land rights. A special relationship had developed between *Jagirdars* and other agrarian groups. The contract for cultivation as a tenant immediately created various obligations. The cultivators were required to fulfill obligations and pay rent and beth-begar, but on the other hand, the landowners had no obligation to furnish production. The peasants were dominated by the landowning community, but sometimes they were exempted from paying usurious amounts and *beth-begar.* In special cases, the *beth-begar* was also payable to individual *Birta* owners and *Jagirdars*, but even if the state exempted them from *beth-begar* obligations, the individual owners did not exempt or lower the *beth-begar* which they were entitled to exact.[46]

The dominant position of landlords and land holding intermediaries had created bitterness in agrarian relations and the peasants had no way to relieve themselves of the burden. Sometimes, the cultivators did not directly pay the *Jagirdars.* They deposited the rent in the *Bakyauta Tahasil Adda* instead of directly paying the *Jagirdars.*[47] Although they could receive the amount, it created disturbances in the relationship between *Jagirdars* and the tenants. In many parts of the country, the

45. 'Order to cultivate *Khangi* land in Pharping, bugmati and Chobhar-1867 V.S...., Poka No. 9, Record Section of the Department of Revenue.
46. On claim of rent by *Jagirdars* 1959 V.S...., Poka No. 159, Record Section of the Department of Revenue.
47. 'On complain against Zamindar's, Poka No. 36, Record Section of the Department of Revenue.

cultivators were exploited and dominated by the privileged classes, who used every means to control them. Sometimes, the cultivators reported such unlawful activities on the part of the privileged classes to the Prime Minister. One of the complaints mentioned that -

> *"... we have no rent dues. But the Zamindar looted the rice crop. He had no right to loot it."*[48]

During that period, the landowners, intermediaries, revenue functionaries and other privileged classes suppressed the peasant community. So, their conditions were most vulnerable as the result of existing agrarian relations. So, there were numerous cases in which *Zamindars* did not consider existing laws or practices and exploited peasants confiscated crops and also evicted cultivators at will. Thus, the tenants or peasant cultivators were subjected to the will of the *Zamindars*.

This type of situation always resulted in the worst kinds of relationship, but occasionally the situation just reversed and the unity and ability of tenants threatened the authority of the *Jimmawals*. The tenants of Rampur and Dadhuwa Kolpu villages once refused to obey the orders of the *Jimmawals*. They were duly appointed during the 'Grand Survey' in 1911 V.S.. (1854 A.D.). The tenants refused to pay *Saunefagu* levy and transplanted paddy seedlings by themselves. The *Jimmawals* could do noting against the tenants, so, they complained to the government to issue an order to legalize their authority. The government ordered the tenants to work according to the *Jimmawals*. If they did not follow the order, they would be punished. The *Jimmawals* were very powerful and played an important role in the relationship with the cultivating community, but sometimes peasants were also united to act against the *Jimmawals*. There were instances in which tenants were united and refused to recognize the *Jimmanwal's*

48. 'On complain against Zamindar's, Poka No. 36, Record Section of the Department of Revenue.

authority. Consequently, they did not pay *Chardamtheki* and managed *Pajani* (appointment or eviction) by themselves. But it is noteworthy that the appointment of the *Jimmawal* required the acceptance of the tenant cultivators of that area. However, they refused to obey them several years after the appointment. But the regime however, considered it to be inappropriate to disobey the existing traditions. So, they were ordered to act as decided during the grand survey of 1847 AD.[49] The orders issued by the premier played a more important role in determining nature of the relationship between landlords and tenants than the existing law did.

The absentee landlords sent their men to different places to reclaim barren land. Later on, the government granted them such land as *Birta*, which the tenants cultivated on contract.[50] Land reclamation had been the top priority. Even before 1846 A.D., the landlords gathered men in their areas and sent them to reclaim new land. The services rendered by citizens during reclamation was sometimes rewarded by the rulers. In many areas reclamation was emphasized by the Ranas. The individual promoters of land reclamation were encouraged to a great extent and were rewarded accordingly.[51] They aere also given various incentives, including, exemption from taxes for several years.

All cultivating tenants were subjected to remain within the grip of landlords. They were even delegated the rights to exact *Dandakunda*, *Marwat, Aputali, Chakchakui* and other levies. The Sirto Rajya paid Sirto tax to the government and enjoyed all possible rights within the territory. The Raja was empowered with hearing suits, except the *Panchakhat*. The inhabitants were

49. 'Order regarding disobey of *Jimmawals* 1920 V.S...., Poka No. 12, Record Section of the Department of Revenue.
50. 'Report on reclamation of land by men of daughter of the HRH Maharaja 1960 V.S...., Poka No. 38, Record Section of the Department of Revenue.
51. On reclamation of land - 1967 V.S...., Jaishi Kotha Poka No. 9, Record Section of the Department of Revenue.

regarded as his subjects. The relationship between the *Raja* and his subjects was a traditional one.[52] This type of system was prevalent in all the former *Baisi* and *chaubisi* principalities during the Rana regime.

The *Jimmawals* and the *Mukhiyas* were responsible cultivating all of the land in their areas and under certain conditions, they were given the right to evict tenants. Usually, the tenants who did not pay rent to the *Jagirdar* were evicted because the *Jimmawal* and the *Mukhiyas* were fully responsible for the payment of rent to the *Jagirdars*. The *Talukdars* (*Jimmawals* and *Mukhiyas*) were very powerful in dealing with cultivators. In the hills, they also dealt with *Jagir* tenants, but sometimes they did not remit arears such as *Serma*, and *Sauneyfagu*, to either *Jagirdars* or *Kaushi Tosha Khana* (Department of Expenditure). In this case, it was obvious that the government would replace him. The main duties of a *Jimmawal* were to promote cultivation, manage the migrants' land and look for revenue defaulters. They were required to appoint tenants considering their current land holding status, their ability to pay rent, and the size of family labour they could provide. They were strictly warned not to default on the *Jagirdar's* share even in the event of natural calamities.[53]

They used every means to avoid such unpleasant situations, but sometimes, they compelled tenants to till the land and pay rent. In *Raikar*, the tenants usually rented land for cultivation to sub-tenants. This sometimes created clashes between them as to who held occupancy rights. The concerned authority also did not use the law uniformly in settling disputes. Even the *Rukkas* were issued in such cases, but sometimes contradicted other cases of a similar nature. The land rented for cultivation

---

52. '*Rajya Birta* to Baghangi Raja Jaya Prithvi Bahadur Singh 1960 V.S..., Poka No. 38, Record Section of the Department of Revenue. also see - '*Rajya* grant to Bajura Raja 1959 V.S...., Jaishi Kotha Poka No. 159, Record Section of the Department of Revenue.
53. 'Order regarding dismissal of *Mukhiyali* and eviction of tenants 1919 V.S..., Poka No. 12, Record Section.

on a contractual basis was not to be registered in the names of cultivators.[54]

The sub-tenants or the sharecroppers had to fulfill all obligations, financial and material, of the owners. The occurrence of clashes on a particular piece of land ended the relationship between the *Raikar* tenants and sub-tenants. These kinds of problems were also witnessed in the *Kipat* tenure. There was fierce competition to obtain land for cultivation, as it was the only means of capital formation in rural Nepal. Therefore, it was more profitable for owners to rent land for cultivation than to cultivate by themselves. Even the tenants of different tenures rented it to cultivators for higher bids, which automatically included various other *Salamis* (tribute) and *Koshelees* (gifts). But sometimes the subtenants who held land from tenants some times claimed occupancy rights which consequently, increased the number of land disputes in the courts (Adalats or Dhansar).

Sometimes, the *Jimmawals* even looked for chances to seize land and deprive tenants of their right to cultivate. Most of the *Jimmawals* were irresponsible and acted as if they only intended to exploit the peasantry but not to help them. Their interests were completely contrary to the welfare of the peasant cultivators. Although the Rana regime was based on a feudal system, thereby protecting the interests of the landed aristocracy, the administrators in districts or in the centre (the Rana officers of different categories) ordered to the concerned offices to settle cases within a shorter period of time and regulate land occupancy and soon. In all such cases, they were strictly advised to test all possible evidence and witnesses on the basis of existing Ain. Such orders were frequently issued by the premier, Commander in Chief, and Commanding Generals as needed.[55]

---

54. 'Order regaring the calshes between tenant and sub-tenants in *Raikar* aldn 1931 V.S...., Poka No. 36, Record Section of the Department of Revenue.
55. 'Rukka on *Kipat* tennure 1931 V.S..., Poka No. 36, Record Section of the Revenue Department.

— 'On land claimed by cultivators 1931 V.S..., Poka No. 36, Record Section of the Department of Revenue.

The tenants in Nepal had paid not less than 50% of the gross produce since the 14th Century. Sharecropping was called *'Adhiyan'*, and the cash rent was called *'Mahasuli'*.[56] In the nineteenth & the twentieth Centuries, the sharecropping tenancy was very common in Nepal, but in the Tarai, rent was assessed on proportional basis, as one sixth of the gross produce. This was the governments' share whereas the landowners or the *Talukdars* exacted one half of the product. Along with the rent assessment system, the numerous taxes, *Rakams, beth-bagar* and *Jhara* were significant factors in the relationship between landlords and tenants.

The tenants are called *'Mohi'* in Nepali. In fact, they had no rights on the land they cultivated. Their occupancy rights evolved from 1823 V.S.. in the Tarai and 1868 V.S.. in the hill region. During the Ranas' rule, it was a customary practice that cultivators who cultivated land for 2 years and paid rent regularly had the right to occupy it.[57] In some places, the tenants sold their cultivation rights but cultivated the same piece of land as the sharecropper. But in either case, the payment of rent remained as usual. Around 1951 A.D., the *Mohiyani* (tenancy) was legally transacted with the involvement of money. Tenancy rights were guaranteed for the first time by the Tenancy Rights Acquisition Act of 2008 V.S.. (1951 A.D). According to the act, the tenants who cultivated land throughout the year 2007 V.S.., which belonged to the landowners on the basis of *Bataiya, Ukhada, Mankhab, Hunda* (fixed payment in kind), *Kutbali* and payment of rent in kinds would give them tenancy rights or *Mohiyani*. It has created stability in land holding for cultivation. The tenants, here after, were no longer controlled by the landlords, but they were restricted in the sale of such rights.[58]

— 'On land sale without right 1931 V.S..., Poka No. 36, Record Section Revenue Department.

56. Babu Ram Acharya, *Nepal ma Jagga Jamin Ko Byabastha* (Land System In Nepal), (Unpublished manuscript) pp. 3-4
57. *Ibid.*
58. *Nepal Gazette,* No. 22, Part 4, Poush 2008 V.S., pp. 25-28.

During the *Rana regime*, the *Birta* owners enjoyed the right to sell or mortgage *Birta* land. The cultivators did not have any rights on that particular piece of land. The cultivators in most of the tenures were not given significant rights throughout the regime, but this period marked the evolution of tenant's rights.

In fact, agrarian relations were determined by the payment of rent and numerous customary levies as well as by the power, status and role of the revenue functionaries (*Jimidar, Patwari, Jimmawals, Mukhiyas*), absentees (*Birtawar, Jagirdars*), feudal lords and the rulers of the petty states (*Raja-rajauts*), and revenue contractors (*Ijaredars*). The principal concern of the government had been the exaction of revenue. It was also an important determining factor in agrarian relations. The *Muluki Ain* (the Civil Code) of 1910 V.S. (1854 A.D.) is the first written code of Nepal to give some guidance to the agrarian system. Later on, other various laws and regulations such as - *Muluki Sawal*, (Civil regulations), *Madhesh Mal* ko *Sawal* (Revenue Regulations for the Tarai), *Pahad Mal* ko *Sawal* (Revenue Regulations for the hills), *Madhesh Ka Jilla ko Jimidar Patuwari ka Nam ko Sawal* (Regulations for *Jimidar & Patwari* of Various district of ta*rai*), *Jimidar Patuwari Ko Sawal* (Regulations for *Jimidar* and *Patuwari*), *Jimmawali Sawal* (Regulations for *Jimmawals*) and administrative regulations for various districts shaped the relationship between various agrarian groups. Those *Sawals* in general dealt with the rights and duties of respective groups, payment of rent and taxes, collection of revenue, remission, defaulting, eviction of tenants, land reclamation and incentives and so on. In the due course of time, the position of cultivators strengthened and their land rights evolved. During the latter half of the rule, they were permitted to sell cultivation rights in some tenures,[59] but the transfer of rights was not permitted on *Guthi* land. The revenue administration was operated through the Amanti and Thekthiti systems under 28 *Mal Addas* (Revenue Offices) and local village functionaries. The defaulting *Talukdars* or cultivators were tried

59. *Ibid.* p.-52.

on the basis of existing regulations. The *Talukdars* who were entrusted to collect revenue were the *Jimmawal, Mukhiya* and *Subba* and *Rai*. In the Kathmandu valley, the *Mohinaike* worked to identify tenants and collected rent on Jagera land . They transmitted rent to the *Sadardafdar Khana*. During the Rana regime, there was a separate office called *Mohinaike Bandobasta Adda*. The *Talukdars* were fully responsible for the collection of revenue and for dealing with the cultivating tenants on behalf of the government to settle land problems. They had the right to exact *Chardamtheki* and *Sauneyfagu* levies.[60] Their position made them very powerful in villages and provided the opportunity to oppress the peasantry.

During the 'grand survey' of 1925 V.S.. (1868 A.D.), the dry land assessment was made according to the *Bijan* (the seed) system and the cultivators were registered as tenants. They were given *Raitan Purja* (a certificate) in which the amount of revenue was mentioned. It was the situation that paved the way for a face to face relationship between the government and tenant cultivators although they paid rent through the *Talukdars*. In Jumla and adjoining areas, the government faced various land problems. The registered tenants and cultivating tenants differed. It was called the *Khaikar* land. Later on, in 1998 V.S.., all Khaikar land was registered in the name of the cultivating tenants, known as the *Mohi*. In general, the payment of rent and taxes was given greater emphasis than all other factors. The cultivators were required to pay rent by *Chaitra* (mid-April) either to the authorized *Talukdars* or deposit it in the Mal Addas. In the event that they refused to pay, the cultivators were liable for eviction. In this situation, the *Talukdars* were authorized to appoint a new tenant. The *Talukdars* were also ordered to deposit all rent in the *Mal adda* within the month of *Baisakh* (until mid-May). If they did not collect it or defaulted on it, they would be dismissed. There was a legal provision that the

60. Hari Lall, *Pahad Mal Bishya* (On Revenue Matters In The Hill), Kathmandu : Nepali Bhasa Prakasini Samiti, n.d., p.-4.

appointment of the *Talukdar* should be according to the wishes of the cultivators. The newly appointed *Talukdar* had obligations to pay all dues defaulted upon by the former one. He had to pay Rs. 4 as *Salami* which was divided among His Majesty (Rs.2), HRH Sri 3 Maharaja (Rs.1) and the Commander-in-Chief (Rs.1).[61] They collected rent and retained 5% of the total collection as their share. Although they were above the peasantry, with high offices, some of the *Talukdars* were very popular among the cultivators because of their methods in dealing with them, but they had to assist and fully cooperate the local *Mal adda* in taking action against defaulting tenants. The *Byang, Bala, Bosi* and, *Silautey Rakams* were collected every year, otherwise the revenue officer had to pay all the Rakams.[62] This type of collection responsibility kept all the economic units under a tight grip in order to avoid displeasing the regime, so the concerned authorities usually oppressed the cultivators. Sometimes, the *Talukdars* refused to take rent with the intent to evict tenants on charges of defaulting. But there were provisions to punish such usurious *Talukdars*. The *Jimidar-Patuwaris* in the Tarai were ordered not to evict tenants as long as they paid rent and not to oppress them in any way,[63] otherwise they would be fined Rs.50.[64]

The payment of rent had been an important factor in Nepal's agrarian relations during the Rana rule. It made it so that the relationship was exclusively based on economic terms. Therefore, the class of cultivators became an economic unit to produce for the local functionaries, landlords and the government. They were required to pay rent within the

61. *Ibid.* p. 58-59.
62. *Ibid.* p. 38-54.
63. *Madhesh Jilla Jilla Ka Jimidar Patuwari Ka Nam Ko Sawal* (Regulations in the Name of Jimidar Patuwari of Various Districts in the Tarai), Kathmandu : Gorkhapatra Press, 2012 V.S., pp. 38-84.
64. *Madhesh Mal Ko Sawal* (Regulations for the Tarai Revenue offices), Kathmandu : Ministry of Law, Justice and Parliamentary affairs, 2017, V.S. p.-31.

prescribed time.[65] Some acts and government decisions made in 1951 brought significant changes in the nature of agrarian relations which prevailed during the Rana regime. The Tenancy Rights Acquisition Act of 2008 V.S..(1951 A.D.) introduced cultivators' land rights. At the same time, the abolition of *Birta* signified a major change in the relationship although there was a landowner between the government and the cultivators.[66] The *Jagir* tenure was also abolished in the same year, so the *Jagirdars* were no longer part of agrarian relations. This extricated peasants from the economic burden which had been created by the payment of rent in advance to the *Jagirdars*.[67] The major achievement of all those developments was the transformation from a traditional type of agrarian relations to a new one. At that time, the government tried to bring about changes in the nature of the payments as well. In the *Guthi* tenure, it was ordered that the rent would be collected half in cash and half in kind. Before this decision was made, the nature of collection in *Guthi* varied. By 2008 V.S.. all *beth-begar* were abolished, but still the *Talukdars* were functioning in a traditional way. A new incentive of 3 to 5 years rent exemption was declared for newly reclaimed land. Even now, old rules

65. 'Pahad Mal Ko Sawal' (Regulations for hill revenue offices), *Nepal Kanun Patrika,* Vol. 4 Nos . 8 & 9, Kathmandu : The Supreme Court, 2018 V.S., pp. 92-102.
Jimmawali Sawal, *Nepal Kanun Patrika,* Ibid., pp. 151-161.
'Jimidar Patwar Ko Sawal', *Nepal Kanun Patrika,* Vol, 6, No. 1, 2021 V.S., pp. 1-22.
66. *Nepal Gazette,* Part 1, No. 9, Kathmandu, 15 Ashwin, 2008 V.S. p-3.
67. The rent in *Guthi* land was paid both in cash and kinds. The system was :
His Majesty's *Guthi* -¾ in kinds and ¼ in cash at the rate of 3 *Pathi 2 Mana* for Rs. 1
Mana *at Rs* 1
Machhindra Nath, *Guthi :* Payment in kinds Rs. 1 = 2 *pathi* 4 *mana* paddy.
—*Nepal Gazette,* part. 4, No. 30, Falgun 2008 V.S., (March 1951), Kathmandu, pp. 55-56.

are functioning in some districts where land is not surveyed according to the Act of 1964 and the Land Revenue Act is not applied.

The Royal proclamation of 2012 V.S.. also retains great importance in the study of the agrarian history of Nepal. It was intended to bring immediate relief to the peasants.

This proclamation brought about significant changes in the nature of agrarian relations. The important declarations are[68]—

— The landowners were not entitled to exact more than 50 % of the gross produce as rent.
— The interest rate was fixed at 10 % both in cash and in kind loans.
— The interest on seeds was reduced to 25 % from 100 %
— All customary taxes and Salimis were declared illegal to exact. Punishment was decided according to the amount of tax exacted afterwards.
— The cultivators who cultivated land for 2 consecutive years were entitled to tenancy rights. A Landowner could not evict tenants until they paid the stipulated rent regularly.
— None of the landowners could keep land uncultivated for 3 years without appropriate reasons. Under these conditions, the government would rent land for cultivation to other tenants.
— The 10 % land tax in Birta was abolished.
— The landowners were compulsorily required to provide receipts to the tenants at the time of rent payment.
— Restrictions were placed on land subletting without the prior approval of the landowners.
— To keep records of landlords and tenants throughout the kingdom.
— The income tax on Birta rent was levied from 5 % to 27.5 % according to the amount.

68. Grishma Bahadur Devkota, *Nepal Ko Rajnaitik Darpan* (Political Mirror of Nepal), Kathmandu : Dhruba Bahadur Devkota, 2036 V.S., pp. 316-317.

The agrarian relations during the Rana regime showed very few changes in their traditional nature, but after 1951 various changes were brought about in agrarian relations through the enactment of different laws, government decisions and proclamations. Such changes were further advanced by the long awaited Land Reforms Act in 1964.

* * *

CHAPTER IV

STATUS OF THE CULTIVATORS

The discussion of the status and role of all the involved parties in agriculture and the material benefits they accrued is very important in this kind of study. Therefore, in a historical context, the rights and status of individuals in agriculture reflected the ambiguity which pervaded agrarian relations. The existing rent-credit squeeze had been the basic theme of agrarian relations in Nepal throughout the ages. The agrarian structure was traditional and almost completely dominated by the rights of the landowning elite. The land tenure system in Nepal represented a coalition between the aristocracy, bureaucracy, and the local landowners.[1] At the bottom of the structural hierarchy, there was the cultivating class of peasants and the landless labourers. The peasant community played a significant role in the production process, but they were almost ignored by the elite groups, who enjoyed land rights. The peasants' land rights were well defined. In the nineteenth and twentieth centuries, there had been a customary practice which placed restrictions on the eviction of peasants or tenants so long as they paid rent, taxes and levies regularly. If landowners violated the rule, they were to be punished in proportion to the total

1. John T. Scholtz, "Policy Process and Rural Development : A Study of Land Reforms in Nepal", Unpublished Ph.D Dissertation Submitted in The University of California, Berkeley : 1977. Cited from : IDS, *Rural Landlessness in Nepal,* Kathmandu : Integrated Development Systems, 1985, p. 6.

land yield. On the contrary, bidding was also permitted in *Birta, Guthi*, and *Kipat* tenures. But, the resident cultivators were not supposed to be evicted by the landlords, village headmen and other concerned authorities were to appoint non-resident cultivators.[2] At that time, this practice was the only incentive for cultivators to remain on the land, but there was a way out on Birta, Guthi and Kipat land. The owners of those tenures were permitted to evict tenants if the higher bidders were available. However, tenants who reclaimed land by themselves were protected from such eviction. The Civil Code of 1854 A.D. protected them against forceful eviction and permitted them to retain cultivation rights, but it was the responsibility of the cultivators to bear all incurred expenses and fertilize land to facilitate good cultivation. However, the actual cultivators were not registered in the revenue records. It was the landowners who was registered as tenants. They were not even given receipts upon payment of rent. They lacked documentary evidence to define their rights as well as a proper basis for claiming it. Babu Ram Acharya has noted that the cultivators did not have any land rights until 1823 and 1868 in the the Tarai and hill districts respectively. The statutory settlements were introduced in those years to overcome land problems. On the other hand, there was a standing order that the land should be given to those who paid rent regularly for two years in case there was a quarrel between cultivators about occupying land. Later on, the cultivators on the land of individual owners were permitted to sell occupancy rights. They usually sold it to the land owners and tended to continue cultivating the same plot of land while offering a higher amount of rent.[3] It had been a common practice which was popularly known as the *Magani* system of tenancy. But usually the landowners hesitated to purchase the rights of peasants due to fear of confiscation by the government

2. 'Problems of Land Administration in The Central Hill Region', *Regmi Research Series* Year 13, No. 11, Feb. 1981, p. 172.
3. Babu Ram Acharya, *Nepalma Jagga Jaminko Vyawastha*, (Management of Land in Nepal) (Unpublished Mss), n.d., pp. 8-11.

without compensation. After 1951, a law was promulgated which legally offered to pay compensation for all land acquisitions made by the government. It finally increased transactions involving peasants' land rights. In the hill region, however, it could not become a common practice due to the lack of alluvial soil and higher rates of rent and taxes. In the Tarai region, the landowners were given significant rights comparable to those of the Birta owners, which, to some extent, created dissatisfaction with this situation among the peasant community.[4]

The statutory settlement on land holding during the Rana regime was not very effective. Although there was a law to protect cultivating tenants from eviction if they paid taxes regularly, the land owners evicted them as frequently as possible for higher benefits.

The registered tenants in the *Raikar* land directly dealt with the state in the capacity of landowners. They paid revenue directly to the government. Generally, such *Raikar* tenants rent land for cultivation. This changed their status to that of rent receiving *Raikar* owners from that of mere registered tenants. They enjoyed various land rights. But the proprietary land right were ultimately controlled by the state itself. However, transactions on *Raikar* land did not involve the transfer of proprietary rights. Such transactions involved only occupancy rights. But on the contrary, transactions on Birta land basically involved the land itself because the state granted all rights to the *Birta* recipients. The terminology used for transactions were -*Rajinama* in the *Raikar* and *Farse* in the *Birta* system, which means resignation and settlement or clearance respectively.[5] However in reality, the cultivators were not given significant rights from the early Shah rule until promulgation of the Land Reforms Act in 1964.

The cultivators paid Kut (rent) to the landowners. They

---

4. *Ibid.*
5. Mahesh Chandra Regmi, *Land Tenure And Taxation in Nepal,* Kathmandu : Ratna Pustak Bhandar, 1978, p. 20.

paid excessive rates of *Kut* which valued up to ¾ of the gross product. The rate was usually increased if higher bidders were available, but the *Jagirdars* were not permitted to increase rent beyond the rate mentioned in the *Tirja*. An order issued in 1900 AD indicated that some of the *Jagirdars* increased rent against the law. Therefore, the order which was issued by the Prime Minister following complaints by the *Jagir* tenants restricted rent increases, and it further ordered the Jagirdars to restore the original rates as mentioned in the *Tirja*. In fact, the *Jagir* land was granted on a fixed income basis. Therefore, the *Jagirdars* had no right to increase rent, but in some cases, the actual payment exceeded such limitations. If a *Jagirdar* eas not permitted to collect rent, it was managed by the *Kampu Tirja Adda* (department dealing with the *Tirja* = written evidence, of *Jagirdars*) when a *Jagirdar* was not permitted to collect rents. It was known as the *Khali-Khandey*.[6] The levies regulated in the *Khuwa* villages of high ranking *Jagirdars* were later incorporated into land taxes when the land was returned to the state in the form of Jagera land.[7]

The transfer of the state's rights through *Birta* grants created private land ownership. The *Birta* land which had been utilized for 16 years was legally authorized for continuation of the same even in the absence of documentary evidence. The *Birta* owners were exempted from all in kind taxes to be paid to the government with the exception of the *Pota, Chhap* and *Tiruwa Birtas*. The state, in the capacity of proprietor, handed over all rights to its recipients as *Birta*. Sometimes land transactions between individuals and the state created a special type of *Birta* known as *Kinuwa Bita*, but usually it did not effect on the occupancy rights of the *Birta* cultivators.[8] If a cultivator was issued a *Bharpai* or receipt at the payment of *Kut* rent, it was to become a documentary evidence for registration as a tenant.

6. Hair lall, *Pahad Mal Bishaya* (On Revenue Matters in the Hills), Kathmandu : Nepal Bhasha Prakashini Samiti, 2008, pp. 20-26.
7. Regmi, f.n. 5, p. 23.
8. *Ibid.* p. 23.

However, the tenants on *Birta* tenure lived under miserable conditions in comparison to their counterparts in *Jagir* tenure. The *Birta* owners enjoyed various privileges. They had the rights to improve rent until 1906 A.D. No law was promulgated to control their unlimited rights, which were confirmed at the time of the *Birta* grant. Only in 1906 did the *Birta* legislation prohibit them from charging higher rates than the rates that prevailed on adjoining *Raikar* holdings.[9] At the same time, the grant conditions varied from one type of Birta to another. The transfer of ownership was not permitted in some kinds of *Birta*, whereas some other types of *Birta* were granted with inheritance rights. Thus, the nature of the rights to be enjoyed by the *Birta* owners also varied according to the type of their tenures.

The Rana rulers were more concerned with the collection of revenue from land. Thus, the government placed top priority on cultivating land in order to increase the volume of land revenue.

Since the beginning of the twentieth century, attempts were also made to protect *Jagir* tenants. An order was issued which prohibited the *Ijaredars* from evicting tenants so long as they paid their prescribed rent regularly.[10] Of course, it marked the beginning of peasants' land rights. The individual land owners were also prohibited from hiring peasants who deserted *Mal* lands. The *Birta* owners suffered greatly from the policy, whereas it was favorable for the cultivating peasants. The landowners had no opportunities left to impose unjust terms or exploit them due to the shortage of cultivators. The rights of the state in *Birta, Jagir, Kipat* and *Rakam* tenures was secured in the form of proprietary rights. The ownership rights were handed over to individuals. Thus, they became landowner and many of them did not cultivate it by themselves. Before 1951, the *Raikar* tenants had direct relations with the state, but the

9. Rent and Tenancy Legislation in *Birta* 1906, Cited from-Regmi, f.n. 5, pp. 407-411.
10. 'Landholding in Majhkirat', *Regmi Research Series* 15 : 10, Oct. 1989, pp. 147 and 152.

creation of new *Raikar* land involved two people - the landowners and the cultivators. The former *Birta* and *Rakam* holders were given ownership right, whereas tenancy rights were given to the cultivating tenants. It was protected by the law. Before the abolition of *Birta*, tenancy rights were salable, but the Land Reform Act of 1964 made tenancy indivisible and untransactable. It was transferable only among nuclear family members.

The Land Act 1957 was a landmark in the history of land tenure in Nepal. For the first time in the history, it regulated Kut rent. In the Kathmandu valley, peasants were allowed to pay only Rs. 9.10 instead of paying one Muri of rice. Hence, taxes were lowered by 15%.[11] The Act of 1964 A.D. further lowered it by 29.9%. The tenants cultivating land belonging to individual owners paid excessively higher rates of Kut rent than the rates prescribed for *Raikar* land. Thus, the rate of *Kut* was considered to be exorbitant. Before 1964, the rate was higher than the current rates which constituted from one half to two third of the gross produce. The Rana rulers seldom attempted to protect tenancy rights. The land owners were ordered not to evict tenants and to collect customary rates of rents and levies from *Chhap, Guthi* and *Kipat* holdings. The order of 1873 AD had given occupancy rights to tenants so long as they desired to retain it.[12] In fact, for the first time in the history of Nepal, Bahadur Shah took steps to protect tenancy rights. In 1792 AD, tenancy rights were protected in Kirtipur. Arbitrary eviction was not permitted if the peasants paid rents and taxes regularly, but if they defaulted on payments, they would obviously be evicted.[13] But such protection was not extended to other parts of the country. Even during the twentieth century, tenancy under the state was not better than the situation

11. Regmi, f.n. 5, pp. 32-33.
12. "Tenancy Rights in Dolkha", *Regmi Research Series,* 15 : 2 Feb. 1983, p. 27.
13. C.R. Nepali, *Rana Bahadur Shah,* Kathmandu : Ratna Pustak Bhandar, 2044 V.S., pp. 19-20.

of tenants at will. The presence of privileged classes with their better financial status, such as the *Zamindars* in the the Tarai and the Western Karnali region, left peasants at their mercy. In spite of unfavorable conditions, the peasants more or less enjoyed land rights. These were further strengthened and expanded after the end of the Rana regime.

The Nature of Land Rights:

Kautilya's *Arthashastra* suggested that recipients should not be given land rights except for cultivation rights.[14] The evolution of land rights in Nepal passed through various stages. Before the promulgation of the Land Reforms Act in 1964, only the registered *Raikar* tenants and *Birta* cultivators with documentary evidences were protected from arbitrary eviction. The rights record were also compiled to some extent, but during the second half of the regime, registered *Birta* tenants enjoyed the transfer of rights through transactions. This further contributed to providing a basis for the evolution of land based property rights. Tenurial security, however, was not guaranteed in other tenures. The rights and privileges of cultivating tenants, the peasant community, and landowners varied with each other in different tenures.[15] At the same time, there were provisions and practices which strengthened the owners rights against the interests of the cultivators. The rights record and other supporting situations in various tenures is discussed below.

I. The introduction of the Kut system in the hills created an insecure situation in terms of peasants' cultivation rights, and was a burden for cultivators. The land owners reserved the right to evict tenants if they refused to pay rent offered by other prospective bidders. This was a common practice in Birta. The Kut system ended tenurial stability and cultivation rights although the first civil code guaranteed tenurial security so long as tenants paid the

14. P.N. Vidyalangkar, *Kautiliya Arthashastra* (The Economic of Kautilya), Lahore : Moti Lal Benarsi Dass, 1923, p. 40.
15. IDS, f.n. 1, p. 1.

stipulated rent and taxes dictated by custom or statute.

After compilation of the rights records in *Raikar*, the government granted documentary evidence of titles to peasants.[16] It was a landmark in the history of the evolution of peasants' land rights. The tenants were permitted to sell land under specific conditions. If the plot was favorably located, highly fertile, and had a high level of invested capital and labour, the peasants were allowed to sell their land. Similarly, mortgages was also permitted. After the 1930s V.S.., all peasants cultivating *Raikar* and *Jagir* land received limited property rights.[17] In the *Raikar* and *Birta* tenures, peasants were not permitted to sub let land for cultivation or transfer occupancy rights by any other means. But various legislative measures, such as attempts to protect tenancy, tenants' security, rent collection and the rights of involved parties affected the relationship between the state and the tenants. The *Raikar* tenants later got permanent tenurial rights which were made salable. At the same time, sub-letting land was also permitted. All such practices contributed to uplifting their status to some extent.[18]

The land hòlding rights in Raikar varied from region to region. In the eastern and central hill regions, land property rights were not recognized, so, the sale and purchase of *Raikar* land was prohibited. Their rights were limited only to cultivation and obtaining a share of the produce in most parts of the country.

The *Raikar* tenants obtained land through reclamation or the *Raibandi* system. Occupancy rights were recognized so long as they paid rent, taxes and levies on the basis of existing laws. If they willingly vacated land or defaulted on payments, the right was obviously canceled. Occupancy rights were recognized so long as peasants cultivated the plot and maintained it through the payment of proscribed rent. Generally,

16. Regmi, *Thatched Huts and Stucco Palaces,* New Delhi : Vikas Publishing House, 1918, p. 119.
17. M.C. Regmi, *Land-Ownership in Nepal,* Berkeley : University of California Press, 1976, pp. 174-177.
18. *Ibid.* pp. 170-171.

the *Raikar* tenure was regulated according to the principle that land occupancy rights belonged to the people who reclaimed and used it.[19] Therefore, cultivators' rights were limited to occupation. The transfer of rights necessarily involved the transfer of occupancy rights. The *Raikar* peasants in the central and eastern hill regions were not given property rights in any form, but in the western hills and the Himalayan region, the tenants were permitted to make transactions. Regarding the system in the western hill region, an order mentioned -

> *" In case a cultivator listed in the revenue records does not possess the means to pay revenue due from him, he may sell his land to his relatives."*[20]

In the Tarai, the existing land tenure system did not favour intermediaries, and tax assessment was made directly. However, intermediaries emerged in the Tarai and Karnali region even before 1846. Their land rights were customary. Land ownership and use became separate, and this had immense significance for agricultural development. Land was occupied by non-working land owners, which became a common practice in the country. The owners normally did not cultivate by themselves but rather rented it to the poor peasants who were deprived of means of production. As a result, peasants' rights were limited to cultivation. The cultivators sometimes obtained land from the government for cultivation. In this case, the *patta* (authorized letter) was issued to confirm their cultivation rights. But references have been found that indicate that the local officials sometimes disregarded the *Patta* and evicted tenants in order to rent the plot to higher bidders. At the same time, ownership certificates were also issued to each individual owner, but the rights on the *Raikar* land were not transferable. Property rights were granted to the *Raikar* tenants in the Tarai region after

---

19. Regmi, f.n. 5, p. 265.
20. Yogi Nara Hari Nath, *Itihas Prakash* (Lights on Hisotyr), Book. 2, Vol. 2, Kathmandu : Itihas Prakash Mandal, 2013 V.S., pp. 57-59.

1870. In the eastern the Tarai, permanent occupancy rights were granted to the Patta holders as early as 1793.[21]

The *Chuni ryots* (landholders in the far western hill districts) who were ordinary landholders in the *Karnali* and the Tarai regions, were registered as tax payers in the official records.[22] The status and rights of the *Mohi* in the central and eastern hill regions and the *Chuni Ryots* in the Karnali region differed from each other. Mostly the *Mohi* (tenants) remained only as tenants at will, whereas the *Chuni* Ryots enjoyed private land property rights and tenurial security to a considerable degree in comparison to the *Mohis.*

A complete and reliable record of the rights of parties involved in agricultural activities is a guide for the analysis of agrarian relations,[23] but in Nepal, it was never properly recorded by the Ranas. The revenue settlement was made from 1854 to 1868 AD. An attempt was made to compile records of rights during the revenue settlements. It recorded names of cultivators, land identification and the rates of rent due on the land. A registered tenant in *Raikar* retained land holding rights even while sub-letting for cultivation.[24] The *Ain* of 1935 AD permitted *Raitis* (land holders) and *Zamindars* to transfer land rights through *Rajinamah.* But transfer of property rights was not permitted under any conditions.[25] The land which was already listed in the government records was not available for *Raibandi* (redistribution of land to peasants) because landholding rights were protected on such land. Therefore, the peasants' rights were further consolidated. This was recognized throughout the country since the second half of the 19th

21. Remig, f.n. 17,m p. 173.
22. M.C. Regmi, *A Study of Nepali Economic History,* New Delhi : Manjusri Publishing House, 1971, p. 31.
23. Dietmar Rothemund, 'government Land lord and Tenants in India 1875-1900', repring from *Indian Economic and History Journal,* Vol. IV, No. 4, Dec. 1969, p. 364.
24. 'Jagga Jamin Ko', *Muluki Ain* 1945 V.S. Pt, III, Sec. 2, p. 35.
25. *The Ain - 1992* V.S..., Kathmandu : The Gorkha Patra Press : 1992 V.S. pp. 36-37.

century. The sale and mortgage of *Raikar* land in the the *Tarai* had been permitted since 1870, but before this, residential requirements were imposed upon the transfer of rights in *Raikar* through, sale or mortgage. The *Muluki Ain* of 1888, also recognized the transfer of rights, but it was subjected to the approval of the Talukdars.[26] The transfer of land holding rights was recognized only after 1921, but official registration of transactions was made compulsory. It was intended to avoid all kinds of forgery, and repeated sale of the plot at one time to more than one person.[27] The law termed tenants as Mohi and registered them as tax paying tenants. They were the owners of land in Raikar. Although they were the owners of the land, their rights differed from those of the Birta owners. But Raikar land holding itself was a form of property. The gradual evolution of peasants' rights reached its height when tenancy was protected and total freedom was granted for transferring rights through sale or mortgage, but it was their duty to pay rent regularly. A piece of land was foreclosed only under special circumstances, such as extinction of tanants' family, voluntary relinquishment, or tax delinquency.[28] The evolution of private property rights on *Raikar* did not influence or decrease the rights of the state as the biggest landlord. The state reserved acquisition rights without paying compensation, although the land was registered in the name of a *Mohi*.[29] The status of the state as the ultimate proprietor was maintained intact. If a tenant lets land uncultivated, it was decided to allot it to others. However, there had been practical difficulties in implementing such allotments because the registered tenants paid taxes regularly regardless of cultivation. The state's interest in tax collection was not hampered even at times of crop failure. A report on land tenure conditions (1951 AD) mentioned this situation—

26. 'Jagga Pajani Ko', *Muluki Ain,* f.n. 24.
27. Regmi, f.n. 17, p. 177.
28. *Ibid.,*
29. 'Jagga Jamin Gwoshwara Ko', *Ain,* f.n. 25, p. 70.

> *"... all over the district rich families controlled vast areas of highland tracts and entire hills, and paid a small amount of land tax. They do not reclaim the land nor sublet it for cultivation. On the other hand, a large number of rural people lived under bare subsistence conditions because they had no land for cultivation."*[30]

The government was more or less concerned with the collection of revenue for its own purposes, so, the state was not concerned with cultivation. The end of the Rana regime marked changes in *Raikar* ownership rights too. The registered tenants were given ownership right. They were permitted to collect rent from cultivating tenants as part of the ownership. The cultivating tenants were given only occupancy rights. Prior to 1959, when *Birta* tenure was in effect, the registered *Raikar* tenants were under pressure, under which they possibly lost even rent collecting rights. This was because the state could acquire any plot of land to grant as *Birta* to individuals. This dealt a severe blow to the evolving rights of owners and cultivators on *Raikar* land. This was the system under which the entire concept of tenants' rights on *Raikar* was based. Once land was granted as *Birta*, the rights of cultivating tenants automatically changed. It also determined the relationship between owners and cultivators. Such possibilities of change in relations and tenurial transformations reflected the uncertainty of land rights. It was the Land Acquisition Act (1961) which gave the right to claim compensation in case land was acquired by the state for any purposes.[31]

II. The evolution of property rights had a significant impact on the Birta tenure as well. The state divested rights to individual recipients. The recipients were given land of different categories under various conditions. They were

30. *Land Tenure Condition in Western Nepal,* Kathmandu : Ministry of Land Reforms, 1953, pp. 33-34.
31. "Jagga Prapti Ain 2018 V.S." (the Land Acquisition Act - 1961), *Nepal Gazette,* (Extraordinary), Vol. XI, No. 18, 25 Bhadra 2018.

granted private property rights in *Birta* holdings. They could possess, occupy, hold, transfer, mortgage, subdivide or bequest as specified. The *Birta* owners used land as private property. The state transferred all rights, including proprietary rights in the form of *Birta* grants, but terms and conditions were specified at the time of the grant. Some *Birtas* were granted for ever and were inherited by the successors whereas inheritance, transfer and subdivision was not permitted in some other categories of *Birtas*.

The *Pota, Chhap* and *Tiruwa Birtas* were not inheritable. *Birta* and Tenancy Legislation-1906, attempted to regulate *Birta* taxes and provided security against eviction, but the power of Birta owners and intermediaries exposed the tenants to arbitrary eviction.[32]

The *Birta* system was most unfavourable for peasants. The 1906 legislation of provided security only when they worked directly under the *Birta* owners.[33] The involvement of intermediaries in Birta created more hardships for cultivators and kept them under pressure. However the state did not interfere in relations between *Birta* owners and cultivators regardless of the relationship. The *Muluki Ain* also provided absolute rights and powers to Birta owners. They could evict tenants under certain conditions and increase rent and taxes, which created inconsistencies in the nature of their occupancy. But later, in the hill region, they were restricted from evicting tenants so long as they paid prescribed rent. The rate necessarily corresponded to the rates fixed for adjoining Raikar holding. Sometimes, they were also ordered not to collect higher rates of rent without the prior consent of the *Jimidars*. The mutual agreement between Birta owners and cultivators, or an amount more than 10% higher than the rates prescribed for Raikar holdings was recognized in the Tarai. The *Raja-Rajautas*, too,

---

32. Rent and Tennancy Legislation on Birta, Regmi, f.n. 9.
33. *Ibid.*

were not permitted to collect excessive amounts or to evict tenants from homesteads.[34] Before 1906, the *Birta* owners were permitted to reserve all land for personal use. The *Birta* legislation of 1906 limited the use of land to 5 *Ropani* in the hills and 1.5 *Bigha* in the Tarai region, but acquisitions, which exceeded the specified area of land required the payment of compensation. The use of force to evict tenants was strictly prohibited.[35] The legislation also provided security against arbitrary eviction and strengthened the positions of *Birta* tenants. The registered *Birta* tenants with documentary evidence also appointed prospective cultivators and rented land for cultivation, which was profitable for them. An intermediary called the *Pakhurey Mohi* was actively involved between owners and cultivators. They worked for the *Birta* owners and retained a handsome amount or part of the produce as their share. Sometimes, the *Birta* owners also suffered from a shortage of cultivators. They were prohibited from hiring cultivating tenants from *Mal* lands in order to cultivate *Birta*. This had a direct impact on fixing rent on *Birta* land because the *Birta* owners were usually afraid of loosing cultivators. The competition for *Birta* land for cultivation was not very keen in many parts of the country. So, as a rule, they were compelled to offer incentives to attract cultivators if an adequate number of cultivators was unavailable. Therefore, it was necessary to reduce rent to attract them.

The legislation of 1906 permitted to sell tenancy on the *Rajinama* basis. The purchaser required to pay *Chardamtheki* levy to the *Birta* owner to confirm rights. The transfer of peasants' rights did not necessarily prejudice the rights of the owners. Under normal conditions, *Birta* owners let land for cultivation and accepted *chardamtheki* to ensured their rights. The acceptance of the levy ensured the right and eviction was not permitted for the whole year. One *Sanad* further mentions-

---

34. 'The Rajya of Achham', *Regmi Research Series,* Vol. 15:11/12, December 1966, pp. 190-192.
35. Rent and Tenancy Legislation on Birta, Regmi, f.n. 9.

> *"The owner could not evict tenants for the whole year after acceptance of the Chardamtheki. It is illegal to evict him and let land to others."*[36]

The Land Act of 1957 lowered traditional rates of rent and protected tenancy rights.[37] The rent was fixed at half of the total produce. It further granted occupancy rights in Birta and other tax exempt land to cultivating tenants. The eviction of tenants was permitted only in the event of non-payment of rent, irregular cultivation, and intentional land damage which permanently affected the production process. The act also permitted eviction in order to 5 *Bigha* or 10 *Ropanis* of land for residential purposes in the Tarai and hills. But if landowner was a widow, civil servant, an infant or a recruit in the foreign army, they could use up to 25 *Bighas* or 50 *Ropanis* for cultivation purposes. The ceiling was fixed at 25 *Ropanis* in the Kathmandu valley provided the owner had no land or fell short of the area mentioned.

After the abolition of the *Birta* tenure, all former *Birtas* were converted into *Raikar* under individual ownership. The cultivators of *Birta* were upgraded in order to protect tenancy rights. But before 1959, their interests were totally ignored and unprotected. The intermediaries took all charges on behalf of the *Birta* owners, in some areas, rent collection on *Birta* was entrusted to the *Ijaredars* (contractors). They were restricted from collecting unauthorized payments, bribes or *Salami* (gifts), and harassing people.[38]

---

36. Prohibition to evict tenanct after accepting *Chardmtheki* levy-1909 V.S. Poka No. 34, Record Section of department of Revenue.
37. "Bhumi Sambandhi Ain 2014 (Land Act 1957)", *Nepal Kanun Patrika,* Vol. VI, No. 8, Kathmandu : The Supreme Court, pp. 192-198.
    Also see : *Nepal Gazette,* Pt. VII, No. 7 (Extraordinary), 22 Shrawan, 2014 V.S.
38. 'Revenue Collection in Birta Land 1957 V.S., *Regmi Research Series,* 13:8, August 1981, p. 123.
    Also see : R R C, Vol. 82, pp. 105-107.

The up-to-date records of *Birta* cultivators are not available. The *Birta* owners sometimes imposed excessively high rates of rent or evicted tenants at will irrespective of legal provisions.[39] The *Jimidars*, their co-partners, or creditors who invested money as security against land might pay revenue arrears and be permitted to continue it or take up the land.[40] But immediately after the revolution of 1951, the government imposed a ban on the sale, division, mortgage or bequeathing of *Birta* land and homesteads built in *Birtas*. The *Birta Khareji Adda* (Birta Abolition Office) looked after matters relating to the *Birta* land. But in the same year, the government again permitted transactions of *Birta* land. It also permitted the bequeathing of homesteads and compounds irrespective of size, however resale was not permitted.[41]

The *Birta* owners and other landlords were ordered to issue receipts upon payment of *Kut*, otherwise they would be convicted and punished accordingly. In fact, such receipts had great importance in the granting of rights to cultivators.

III. In Nepal, *Jagir* land was assigned to civil and military personnel instead of cash salaries and emoluments. The landowners' share was granted to them as Jagir. The *Jagirdars* were concerned only with exacting rent and levies from land assigned to them as *Jagir*, and the tenants were not given significant land rights. Before 1854, there was no control over *Jagirdars*' rent increases, although rent was fixed at one half of the produce. The *Jagirdars* enjoyed unlimited power, but the first *Muluki Ain* prohibited them from increasing rent to over one half of the total yield. The re-allotment of *Jagir* land and the

39. *Land Tenure Conditions.....*, f.n. 30, p. 39, and 48.
40. Rent and Tenancy Legislation on *Birta,* Regmi, f.n. 5.
41. The transaction was limited to 25 *Ropanis* in the hills and 25 *Bighas* in the the Tarai.
— Grishma Bahadur Devkota, *Nepal Ko Raijnaitik Darpan* (The Political Mirror of Nepal), Vol. II, Kathmandu : D.B. Devkota, 2036 V.S., pp. 571-572.

payment of the Saykadi levy confirmed tenurial rights, so, eviction was not permitted until the next survey.[42] The *Jagirdars* had to rely on the amount of rent fixed at the time of the grant as mentioned in *Tirja*. They collected rent from tenants who previously cultivated *Jagera* land. There were intermediaries in the *Jagir* land system as well, but neither the *Jagirdars* nor the intermediaries had much interest in improving tenurial conditions or productivity. The tenants also occasionally refused to pay rent at proscribed rates and did not inform them of the division of total produce at the time of harvest. They offered a lump sum amount to the *Jagirdars*. A *Jagir* tenant in Bode village offered 2 to 3 *Muri* of rice for a plot of 5 *Ropanis* instead of dividing the total yield according to the *Adhiyan* (sharing) basis.[43] The influential and rich people at the villages cultivating *Jagir* land usually refused to pay rent at the rate of one half. In western Nepal, rent was collected through the *Thek-Thiti* system. If a *Jagirdar* could not receive rent within a specific period of time , the *Thek-Thiti* arrangement might be canceled and they might collect rent by themselves.[44] The *Jagirdars* enjoyed unlimited rights in Khuwa (homesteads assigned as Jagir) villages although it fell within the area of local *Chaudhuris*. Sometimes, the government also ordered enslaved persons to handed over to the *Jagirdars*.[45]

The *Muluki Ain* of 1854 provided security to tenants against arbitrary eviction. There was already an order for Kathmandu valley, which mentioned—

---

42. *Ibid.*, p. 43.
43. 'Jagir' Rents in Bode Village', *Regmi Research Series* 13:2, February 1981, p. 30
44. 'Revenue Collection in Rolpa', *Regmi Research Series* 10:1 January 1978, pp. 1-6.
45. 'Jagirdari Rights', *Regmi Research Series*, 12:4, April, 1980, p.-63.

> *"So long as the cultivators pay customary dues they shall not be evicted. The land of Jagirdars shall not be seized on the pretext of Jagirdars being outsiders. If any body evict tenants and acquires land, it is illegal and tenants should be re-appointed."*[46]

Eviction was not permitted unless they defaulted rent payments. Re-allotment was permitted if cultivators died, absconded, emigrated or relinquished.[47] The geographical conditions and lack of effective law enforcement systems created problems in the implementation of legal provisions and in monitoring the drawbacks associated therewith. The relationship between *Jagirdars* and tenants was not perfectly regulated. Even during the time of Prime Minister Jung Bahadur Rana, a large number of disputes arose between *Jagir* holding soldiers and cultivators.[48] He attempted to solve the endless *Jagir* disputes. The problems were particularly related to rent increases and the eviction of tenants. Finally, district officials were delegated and granted the power to settle such disputes. At the same time, the tenants were ordered to pay rent regularly. The *Jagirdars* were also ordered to accept *Kut* in the form of what was actually grown in the field. They could not to claim rice although the *Tirja* mentioned *Kut* in form of rice. Remission was granted in the event of crops failure. Damage caused by

46. Royal Order to the Jagirdars of Kiritipur, Thankot and Other villages, 1861 V.S.
    — Cited from-Regmi, f.n. 5, p. 485.
    — Also see-On Eviction of Tenant By A Subba 1931 V.S., Poka No. 36, Record Section of the Department of Land Revenue.
47. 'Appointment of Jimmawals in Thansing', *Regmi Research Series,* 12:12, December 1960, pp. 186-188.
    Also see-Jagir Land Allotment in Rawa Landholding in Majh Kirat, *Regmi Research Series,* 15:10 October 1983, p. 147.
    Land Allotment Regulations-Landholding in Magh Kirat, *Regmi Research Series, Ibid,* pp. 152-153.
48. Padma Jung, *Life of Maharaja Sir Jung Bahadur of Nepal,* Allahabad : The Pioneer Press, 1909, p. 269.

fire or floods was also available for remission.[49] If *Talukdars* evicted tenants illegally in favour of the *Jagirdars*, they were liable to be punished and also to be fined an amount of *Kut* equal to that paid so far.[50] This system was designed to make tenancy secure, but if cultivators did not complain about eviction within a year, they had no right to claim cultivation rights. All rights to hear suits against such disputes was vested in the state . In fact, occupancy rights were secured in Jagir tenure. The Rana government abolished all *Jagir* land in the Tarai in 1853 AD. It was prompted by the realization that -

> *" ... because land in the Tarai region are granted to civil servants and military officials, the amount of revenue deposited in the treasury is meager."*[52]

IV. The occupancy rights in the Guthi tenure (institutional land ownership) permit to inheritance and sub-division.[53] The cultivating tenants were protected from eviction as long as until they paid rent and taxes. An order in 1847 also mentioned such eviction-

> *" The cultivators in Guthi shall not be evicted as long as they pay prescribed dues regularly."*[54]

Although it provided security, it was hardly applied in places where bidding on tenurial rights was regulated. The individual's rights in *Guthi* were limited to occupancy rights. If anybody

---

49. *The Ain of 1992 V.S.*, Vol. III, Kathmandu : Gorkhapara Press, 1992 V.S., pp. 69-73.
50. *Ibid.*, pp. 32-33.
51. Hari Lal, f.n. 6, p. 20.
52. 'Revenue Receipt of the Government of Nepal Durng 'The Nineteenth Century', *Regmi Research Series* 9:8, August 1977, pp. 119-125,
53. *Muluki Ain* 1945 V.S. f.n. 24.
54. Royal Order to "Thakur Singh and other *Guthiyars* in Handigaon. Cited from-Regmi, f..n. 5, pp. 732-733.

reclaimed land, naturally he had the right to occupy and cultivate it, but the sale and mortgage of *Guthi* land was prohibited.[55] Later on, limited mortgaging of *Guthi* was also permitted. The compilation of the record of rights in *Guthi* became the basis for the evolution of private property rights. The restrictions imposed on the transfer of rights could not stop transactions of *Guthi* land. In 1939, actual cultivators were recorded duly and granted ownership rights. In fact, the prevailing system involved two persons at a time on a plot of land along with the institution as the owner of *Guthi* holdings. The registered tenants in *Guthi* were treated as land owners and the other tenant was the cultivator. Both of them had varied land interests. They shared rights in land with each other. The owners ruthlessly exploited the cultivating peasants. The former were fully responsible for making tax payments to the *Guthi* institution. They were also authorized to evict cultivating tenants under specific conditions.[56] The Ain of 1992 V.S.. gave them the discretionary powers for evictions.[57] It was only after promulgation of the Land Act of 1957, that tenancy was protected and rent was regulated in *Guthi*.[58] However, it prohibited the exacting of rent that exceeded the prevailing customary rates. The power of registered tenants to evict cultivators was lowered and eviction was permitted only through the court of law. The Land Reforms Act of 1964, however, did not change the existing *Guthi* system, and did not benefit the actual cultivators of *Guthi* land. The *Guthi* cultivators in the Kathmandu valley paid up to two *Muri* (four mounds) of rice per Ropani as rent to the registered tenants, whereas the share of the *Guthi* institution to be paid by the registered tenants was only one *Muri*. Recently, attempts were made to benefit the actual cultivators by converting Guthi into Raikar and providing ownership rights to the actual cultivators. It changed their status

55. The *Ain 1992, V.S.*, f.n. 25, pp. 1-3.
56. Regmi, f.n. 5, p. 737.
57. *The Ain 1992 V.S...*, f.n. 25. p. 31.
58. "Bhumi Sambandhi Ain 2014", f.n. 37 pp. 192-198.

from that of merely cultivators to that of landowners. The *Muluki Ain*, *Guthi* legislation of 1923, the Sawals etc. dealt with the rights of the involved parties, rent payment, eviction and tenancy security, the transfer of rights and so on in Guthi.[59] It also regulated existing agrarian relations in the *Guthi* tenure during the Rana rule.

The political changes in 1951 marked an epoch in the study of agrarian relations. The government was pressurized to promulgate land laws to correct defects in the agrarian structure. The Land Act of 1957 and its amendments in 1959 and 1961 hold great importance in the study of peasant's land rights. The laws promulgated until 1964 dealt with rights of the owners and the cultivators, and attempted to bring about reforms in the system and regulate relations between agrarian groups and the state. The abolition of traditional land tenures such as the *Jagir, Birta, Kipat* and *Rakam* tenures also brought about significant changes in the traditional agrarian set up and in agrarian relations. At present, there are three kinds of cultivated land in Nepal—

— The *Raikar* or the *Mal* land in which revenue is paid to the government by the owners who are registered as tax paying tenants in cadasters.

— Land under tenancy -the tenant cultivators paid rent to land owners in kind in the place that he designated. A negligible percentage goes to the government treasury in the form of rent and taxes paid by the owners. The government gave this right of revenue collection to village development committees and municipalities.

— The *Guthi* land : Rent is payable to the *Guthi* corporation or to religious and charitable institutions, but the registered tenants who collected *Kut* from cultivating tenants retained almost half of the amount. Now, considerable areas of *Guthi* are being converted into *Raikar*.

---

59. Such *Sawals* include—
Muluki Sawal, Madhesh Mal Ko Sawal, Pahad Mal Ko Sawal, Madhesh Jila Jila Ka Jimidar Patwari Ka Nam Ko Sawal etc.

During the post 1951 era, the agrarian relations were remarkably transformed. The Royal Declaration of 1955 proved to be a milestone in the evolution of peasants' rights on the land which they cultivated. The Royal Declaration emphasized that—

— All the customary levies were declared illegal.
— The Kut should not exceeds one half of the total production.
— To grant tenancy rights to those who cultivated land regularly for two years.
— The eviction of tenants was not permitted until they paid customary rent rates.
— It was compulsory to issue a receipt upon the payment of rent , and
— To compile the peasant - cultivators record.[60]

The royal declaration proved to be very significant in tenancy protection and rent collection, but on *Birta* land, the transfer of tenancy rights through sale was withheld without prior consent. There was no restriction on tenancy rights before 1957, but the Land Act of 1951 was not duly implemented. On the other hand, the Agricultural Rent Act of 1955 also levied a fine equivalent to the amount of Kut on those who failed to pay rent as prescribed by the law.[61] The Land Act of 1957 has been considered to be one of the most significant steps in the agrarian history of Nepal. It controlled the traditional rate of rent which was profitable for the absentee landlords, non-cultivating owners, and intermediaries. It attempted to regulate rent and tenurial security. Agrarian relations, in terms of rent and its collection, had been regulated by traditional factors. The Rana rulers favoured the landed aristocracy, squire and local gentry for political reasons, which was the main factor

60. "Royal Proclamation", *Nepal Gazette*, Pt. X, N. 20 (Extraordinary), 22 Poush, 2017, p. 4.
61. "Krishi Sambandhi Bali Bishyako Ain" (the Agricultural Rent Act 1955), *Nepal Gazetter*, Pt. IV, No. 44, 6 Ashad, 2012 V.S., pp. 4-6.

that caused the rulers to ignore the cultivating peasant community for centuries.

The act of 1957 fixed rent at the rate of one half of the total production. The land owners were no longer permitted to collect rent exceeding legally prescribed rates. The legal provision was that the lowest rate was to be used, and eviction was permitted only through the courts of law.[62] In some tenures, the law brought owners and tenants into a face-to-face relationship. The act also limited the amount of land that was to be claimed by the owners for personal use. In spite of such reforms, the law of 1957 hurt the interests of the cultivating classes. The legislation of 1906 had already guaranteed rights in the form of a minimum of 2 *Bighas* and 2 *Ropanis* of land in favour of the cultivators, obviously with the objective of guaranteeing them a means of subsistence and protecting them from displacement.[63] However, the law was no longer concerned with such problems, and no longer protected them from the consequences of land reclamation, so, there was still a high risk of displacement from the villages. Therefore, it will be more appropriate to evaluate the act of 1957 in terms of the rights of peasant cultivators. The law abolished all kinds of customary levies and the *Beth Begar*. The land owners were ordered to issue receipts to peasants upon payment of rent because most of them did not issue receipts. The peasants had the right to deposit *Kut* in the *Mal Adda* in case the landowners refused to collect it or issue receipts.

The cultivators who had cultivated land for at least for two consecutive years were recognized the protected tenants. The peasants' right were decided according to oral or written agreement.[64] On the contrary, land regulations in 1960 allowed the eviction of tenants for the purpose of making homesteads.[65]

62. "Bhumi Sambandhi Ain 2014", f.n. 37, pp. 192-198.
63. Regmi, f.n. 5, pp. 331-333.
64. "Bhumi Sambandhi Samsodhan Ain 2016 V.S. (the Land Act First Amendment 1959), *Nepal Gazetter,* Pt. IX, No. 19, 1 Poush, 2016 V.S.
65. The Land Regulations 1960.

This was considered to be a threat to tenants' security. Earlier, the law of 1957 allowed certain landowners to evict, but the ceiling was fixed at 25 *Ropanis*, 50 *Ropanis* and 25 *Bighas* in the Kathmandu valley hills and the Tarai regions respectively. Before 1957, a limitation was imposed on eviction requiring for the peasants to have at least 2 *Ropanis* or 2 *Bighas* of land after eviction so they would not be landless.[66]

The amended version of the Land Act of 1957 also ignored the peasant's interests, although it proved to be a significant step in the evolution of peasants' land rights. In 1962, the third amendment of the act fixed rent at new rates and again guaranteed tenancy security. The rent rates were fixed as follows—[67]

The rate was 2 *muri* 3 *pathi*, 18 *pathi* 6 *mana*, 13 *pathi* and 8 *pathi* 5 *mana* on irrigated lands, and 10 *pathi* 1 *mana*, 7 *pathi* 2 *mana*, 4 *pathi* 3 *mana*, and 2 *pathi* 7 *mana* on dry land in *Abal, Doyam, Sim* and *Chahar* grades of land. Normally, 4 *mana* of rice is equivalent to one kilogram.

The promulgation of the land reform act in 1964 proved to be a landmark in the agrarian history of the country, although it did not introduce complete reforms. Certainly, the act brought about significant changes in the traditional agrarian system of Nepal and proved to be a major relief for the peasantry. It also granted rights to different agrarian groups. Rent control and tenancy security were significant changes which were brought about by the act of 1964, but it still allowed the continuation of traditional land ownership rights to evict tenants for homestead purposes.

The registered *Raikar* tenants were given ownership rights. The Land Reforms Act also clearly defined land property rights. The *Raikar* tenants enjoyed such rights as well. On the other hand, the tenants under individual landowners were originally

66. *The Ain 1992* V.S., f.n. 25, pp. 29-42.
67. "Bhumi Sambandhi Tesro Samsodhan Ain 2018 V.S." (the Land Act third amendment 1962), *Nepel Gazette,* Pt. XI, No. 40 (Extraordinary), 24 Magh, 2018.

given property rights only on 1/4 of the total area they cultivated,[68] but in recent times, the rate has risen to one half in practice regardless of the existing law. The tenants used to receive 1/2 of the total area upon the division of landed property as part of their ownership rights if it was to be divided. In the event of refusal on the part of the tenants, the landcould not be divided, and the use of force was strictly prohibited. This is particularly applied on urban or sub-urban homestead land, but the ratio of 1/4 is still in effect on agricultural land in the hill and Tarai regions. In recent years, many people felt that the Land Reforms Act of 1964 had to be amended in order to ensure land rights and regulate relationships. Thus, a political competition between the Nepali Congress and the Nepal Communist Party (UML) finally resulted in the promulgation of the land Act amendment in 1995 which ensured that peasants are given one half of the total area as their share of ownership rights.

The Reaction Against The old System:

Although Nepal witnessed harmonious relationship between major and minor ethnic groups, the relations between members of different socio-economic groups was not always peaceful. The centuries old relationship between different classes in the society sometimes resulted in struggle for land rights. In fact, exploitation by the privileged classes has created violent clashes in different parts of the country at different times.

In Eastern Nepal, the transfer of land holding rights on Kipat land and legal permission to convert it into *Raikar* under certain conditions in 1886 made the local Brahmans able to occupy Kipat in a larger scale. They continued to take land from the Limbus while extending loans.[69] The rural poverty in the Limbuwan area made the Brahmin money lenders very influential in the region. Most of the areas came under their control through possessory mortgage. Consequently, the

69. Lionel Caplan, *Land and Social Change in Eastern Nepal, IBerkeley : University of California Press*, 1970, pp. 91-92

dissatisfied Limbus organized a movement which resulted in the killing of many Brahmin money lenders, but the Rana government quickly suppressed it.[70]

The exploitation of the peasant community was very similar throughout the country. The existing regulations, interests of the landed aristocracy, dominant position of the privileged classes, lack of laws protecting tenants & cultivators etc. contributed to the rising dissatisfaction among the peasant community. The traditional land holding rights of the ethnic minorities passed into the hands of the rich money lenders.[71] The rights of the *Chepangs, Tharus, Limbus, Sunuwar* and other ethnic groups passed in the hands of influential local functionaries through usurious methods.[72] The influx of *Brahmin* and *Chhetry* settlers in and around the *Tharu* settlements in the Tarai finally destituted 15,000 *Tharu* families in the Dang valley alone. Thus, not only it effected their economic activities but also created a cultural identity crisis.[73] Obviously, many of them turned to political activism to protect their rights and themselves against oppression. Thus, there were violent clashes between the Tharu peasants and landlords on the question of land ownership in Dang district, which later extended to other areas. In fact, the peasant community was extremely exploited throughout the Tarai region. The existing system of agriculture and agrarian relations contributed to the

---

70. B.P. Uprety, "Limbu-Brahman Interreletionship in Limbuwan Nepal", Unpublished Ph.D. dissertation, University of Wisconsin at Madson, 1975, pp. 139-172.
71. N.K. Rai, *The people of Stone—The Chepanags of Central Nepal,* Kathmandu : Centre for Nepal and Asian Studies, 1985, pp. 43-48.
72. For details on Sunuwar Society see :
    Alain Fournier, "The Role of Priest in The Sunuwar Society", In Jim Fisher (ed.), *Himalayan Anthropology,* The Hague : Mouton, 1978, pp. 167-178.
    For details on the chepanges see : Genesh Man Gurung, *The Chepangs : A Study in continuity and Change,* Kathmandu: Publishes 1988, pp. 41-50.
73. T. Cox, "Land Rights and Ethnic Conflict in Nepal", *Economic and Political Weekly,* Vol. 25, No. 24-25, June 1990, p. 1318.

creation of a large number of radical and violent movements. In the central the Tarai, the peasant movements broke out mainly because of exploitation and for acquisition of tenancy rights after 1951. The peasant movements in Siraha, Rautahat, Dhanusha Bara Sunsari and Morang districts were very much influenced by the Marxist ideology, and proved to be a serious blow to the exploitative *Zamindars*.[74] Similarly, a large number of movements were organized by the *All Nepal Peasants' Party (ANPA), Akhil Nepal Kisan Sangh* (ANKS), *Bhumi Jiwi Sangh (BJS)* and others in the the Tarai right after 1951. But in the Kathmandu valley, peasants' interests were represented by the *Krishi Sudhar Sangh* (Agricultural Reforms Association) and *All Nepal Peasants' Purification Committee (ANPPC)*. The historically important movements organised in the the Tarai are are as follows- *Katan Bandh* (No harvest) and no grain export movement - *Jhapa, Tamsuk Chyatne Andolan* (Bonds tearing movement) in the central Tarai districts of Saptari, Mahottari, Sarlahi, Rautahat, Parsa and Bara, the no grain storage movement (in *Palpa* and *Pyuthan*, *Parsa* and *Bara*), movement against the *Gol Rakam*, the anti-exploitation movement, the movement for tenancy rights, and the one third Kut Movement in Kathmandu.[75] The *Kisan Majdoor Party* in Bhaktapur launched a movement called the crop harvest movement against the feudal system in 1971 under the leadership of Narayan Man Bijhukchhen 'Rohit'.[76] The Nepali Congress also led some of the movements in different parts of the country. The important movements led by the Nepali Congress were *Tirobandi Andolan* (Fixed rent movement), and the *Suddhikaran Kisan Sangh* (Purification Peasants Association) which also led movements for tenancy rights and exemption from rent due in Kathmandu valley. The movements against landlords in Rajapur (Bardia-1952) and the Nuwakot Uprising (1959) were

---

74. Ram Bhandur Jyapu, *Nepal Kisan Andolan Ko Ek Jhalak* (An Outline of Peasant Movements in Nepal), Kathmandu : Yuba Sahitya Gosthi, n.d., pp. 1-50
75. *Chhalphal Weekly*, 9:14, Kathmandu ; 2048 V.S.
76. *Ibid.*

organized by the local peasants without the involvement of any political parties. In fact, all those movements were the result of political changes and impact of the prevailing system.

The rebellion led by Bhim Dutta Pant in western Nepal was also a kind of peasant movement blended with politics. Even during the Panchayat rule, there were various peasant movements against the government and landlords. In 1966, the peasants resisted the compulsory saving scheme. The activities of peasants in Butwal in this regard is noteworthy. Similarly, the *Jhora Andolan* (1968-70), *Jhapa Kisan Andolan* 1971 and *Lumbini Kisan Andolan* (1968-74), movement against usurious interest rates in *Kabhre- Timaj* 1966, the *Jugedi Kisan Andolan* (1976-77) to capture landlords' granaries and distribute their contents to the poor, the Sarlahi Movement-1976, the Sindhupalchowk movement against higher interest rates -1979, the *Bani Sangharsha* of Dhanusha (movement for wages) 1969-70, the Piscar movement - 1980, and the demands of Peasants of Chitwan -1986 are all listed among the documented peasant movements. Furthermore, there were hundreds of other movements organized during 1950s, both in the hill and the Tarai districts. Most of these movements have great historical importance.[77] All the peasant movements in Nepal were organized primarily due to economic exploitation, the need to

77. During the democratic movement in 1951, the peasants revolted against the *zamindars* in the areas, as a result of ruthless exploitation by the latter. The peasants worked in th efileds their whole lives in order to extricate themselves from the burden of debt, but they were never able to rid themselves of it, even if the amount of det had been insignificant. The peasant leaders were determined to eradicate exploitation and improve conditions for the peasant community. It has been revealed that the landholdrs in the Lumbinin area and other parts of the western the Tarai ruthlessly expolited the cultivating tenants. Once they fell into debt, they could never be free from it., The existing system of *Kamaiya* (bonded labour) also supports this statement.

— Kashi Prasad Shrivastav, *Nepal Ki Kahani* (The Story of Nepal), Delhi : Atma Ram and Sons, 1955, pp. 112-124.

protect land rights, and the authorities' refusal to protect peasants' interests and tenancy rights. In most cases, the movements were organized by banned political parties such as the Nepal Communist Party (NCP) and the Nepali Congress (NC). The government at that time did not listen to the peoples' demands. Therefore, movements were suppressed in favour of the squires, local gentry and the landed aristocracy. Usually, the participating peasants were brutally executed. Nevertheless, the movements played significant role in shaping agrarian relations and politics in the country. Even after the promulgation of the Land Reforms Act of 1964, the existing agricultural system in the country and the peasant community faced various problems. The problems in agrarian relations and the question of land rights, the payment of *Kut* and its ratio to total production all contributed to the peasants' dissatisfaction. Therefore, they demanded reforms on their behalf.

The Rana regime was marked by unequal relationships in the agrarian sector. The peasant community served the interests of the upper classs and privileged community, against which it was very difficult to resist. Medieval feudalism also prevailed in agriculture in modern times, and this very situation that compelled the peasantry to live in bare subsistence.

The peasants were not given land rights throughout the Rana regime. The existing rates of rent taxes and levies, the interest and power of the landlords, debt-credit arrangements etc. all played a vital role in agrarian relations.

It is of course, significant to analyze the practice of customary levies during the Rana regime. It helps to analyze the peasantry's conditions, domination by the privileged classes, and the nature of agricultural relationship.

The Burden of Customary Levies :

The agrarian history from 1846 to 1951 mainly focuses on the exaction of numerous taxes and levies which were paid by the peasant community in addition to the regular rent payments. Most of the customary levies were paid for nothing; therefore, it proved to be an extra financial burden for the toiling peasantry. The exaction of levies represented the dominance of the landowning elite over the entire peasant community. They were required to pay levies regularly in order to continue to cultivate a particular piece of land.

During the Rana regime, numerous levies were associated with agriculture. There were almost 360 types of agro-commercial levies until that time, and some 150 types of levies were in effect at the time of the Ranas. Every peasant household paid 3 to 5 kinds of levies regularly,[78] for an instance, the Sauney-Fagu, Chardam Theki and the Ghiukhaney levies, which were paid regularly by most of the cultivators. The rates of levies, however, varied from place to place.[79]

During 1840s, the rates of the Sauneyfagu levy were as follows—[80]

Table No : 3

Rates of Sauneyfagu for different communities

Payers	Sauney Levy	Fagu Levy
Birta owners	2 Ana (Rs. 0.08)	2 Ana (0.08)
Amal-Umrao	4 Ana (Rs. 0.16)	4 Ana (0.16)
Jamdar,Major,Adjut.	3 Rs.	2 Rs.
Common people	1 Ana (0.04)	1 Ana (0.04)

This table shows that in spite of being the actual beneficiary of the existing agrarian system, the *Birta* owners paid just a small amount of *Sauneyfagu*. The amount was only Rs. 0.02, the peasants paid the same levy at the rate of Rs. 0.04, which was double the amount paid by the cultivating families. The government, however, did not want to antagonize the landed elite, for the sake of political benefits.

78. K.N. Banstola, "Land Revenue Administration in Nepal," (Ph.D dissertation) Poona : Poona University, 1985, pp. 439-440
79. 'Tax collection in the Jagera Land' *Regmi Research Series,* Year 12, No. 6, June 1980, Kathmandu : p. 92.
80. 'Rates of *Sauney Fagu* Levies', *Regmi Research Series,* Year 14, No. 7, July 1982, Kathmandu : pp. 102-103.

In addition to the *Sauney Fagu* levy, a homestead tax called the *Serma* was also charged. The former was charged on each household, whereas the latter was based on rough estimate of the size of the homesteads.[81] The peasants in the Rana period were obliged to pay a multitude of levies, such as poll taxes or taxes based on caste, ethnic origin and occupation.[82] In addition to these taxes, the landowners also exacted customary gifts. In the Kathmandu valley, the peasants had to offer seasonal vegetables, fruits, grains, butter, milk, curd, fuel wood, labourers etc. to the landlords and the money lenders to secure their good-will.[83] Sometimes the value of such gifts exceeded the actual amount of levies. At the same time, it was the duty of the local peasants to feed government functionaries, visiting dignitaries and troops.[84]

The landlords who had the right to dispense justice collected the *Asmani* levy, which was collected in advance from each household. The collection of taxes, rent and levies was entrusted to certain individuals in different places, and the excess amount was not transmitted to the government.[85] However, the Ranas also declared to the contrary, that any person who oppressed the Ryots, acted beyond the limits of his authority, and extorted payments from the owners of existing homesteads in order to compensate for the revenue lost on depopulated homesteads would be declared guilty.[86]

---

81. Regmi, f.n. 16, p. 58.
82. *Ibid.*
83. Facts revealed from interviews with elderly persons who had witnessed the system during the Rana regime and also worked in the Land Reforms Deparment.
    — Interview with Padma Bahadur Budhathoki, a peasant leader of ANSKS on 2045.103 V.S.
    — Interview with Arjun Bahadur Thapa, an officer in the Land Reforms Department on 2046. 12.7 V.S.
84. Regmi, f.n. 16, p. 60.
85. 'Excessive taxation', *Regmi research Series,* Year 12, No. 12, December 1980, Kathmandu : p. 177.
86. 'Unfair Collection Procedures', *Regmi Research Series,* Year 12, No. 12, December 1980, Kathmandu p. 117.

Rent Collection and Disputes :

Various historical documents in the Records Section of the Department of Revenue revealed the nature of disputes and petitions filed against unfair collection methods. This had been the major cause of disputes between owners and cultivators. Sometimes, the peasants requested for the local authorities to intervene in their cases, but it was never a common practice in the country. Although the peasants were largely controlled by the landed aristocracy, these cases provided information about the rent collection methods that were used at that time. In most cases, the central government ordered the local authorities to settle disputes thorough existing laws - otherwise they would be punished.

The individual absentee landlords appointed intermediaries to collect rent and levies, the land tax was collected by the local revenue functionaries on behalf of the government. They employed various tax collection methods, but there are examples of reports against illegal tax and rent collection practices.

The government took the toughest measures against default on the part of the revenue contractors.[87] It was expected to clear all due taxes as soon as possible or risk punishment. In the western region, the government was ordered to remit all land taxes within the same year.[88] In 1957 V.S.., a survey was conducted in Achham and Doti districts, where tax was assessed on the basis of both the *Haley* (*Patey-Kodaley* also = plough) and the *Bijan* (seed) systems. The act of tax collection was entrusted to the *Talukdars*.[89]

Generally, the individual landowners exploited the cultivating peasants as much as possible. There were cases in which the landlords or the appointed intermediaries collected

87. On Matters of Revenue Defaulting-1959 V.S., Poka No. 159, Record Section, Department of Revenue.
88. Order to Remit Land Taxes 1959 V.S..., Poka No. 159, Record Section Department of Revenue.
89. An Order to Access Land Tax in Doti and Achham 1959 V.S..., Poka No. 180, Record Section of the Department of Revenue.

Pota tax from the sharecroppers in addition to collecting rent at the rate of one half of the gross product.[90] For the cultivators the payment of half of the produce for rent as well as the prescribed amount of *Pota* tax was unacceptable, because it was very difficult for them make such payments.

The landowners were permitted to rent land for cultivation under written contract. In some cases, the landlords breached the contract and demanded rice in *Kut*, although the contract specified that the payment of rent was to be in cash. This was a common practice in the Tarai districts.[91] Such demands did not favour the cultivating classes. Thus, the peasants usually demanded justice from the local government authorities.

In fact, the existing customary and statutory practices, rates of rent and collection methods were exploitative in nature against the entire peasant community in the country, and had a profound impact on the economic life of the cultivators. But there was no alternative to following the customs, statutes or demands of the landlords in order to retain cultivation rights. If they did not comply, they were evicted and deprived of their cultivation rights.

The existing systems, traditional land holding practices and exploitation by the cultivating community finally led to the establishment of various peasant organizations to demand and protect peasants rights. Various movements were organized in different places and were led by different organizations. Such movements were sometimes violent but finally benefited the peasant community. Gradually, they began to receive more land rights, rent reductions etc. Of course, those movements discouraged landlords from exploiting the peasantry.

Thus, there is a correlation between prevailing agrarian conditions and organised movements. The centuries old

90. Petition on Payment of Rent and Excessive collection of Tax in Sharecoropping Land 1931 V.S..., Poka-36, Record Section Department of Revenue.
91. Order on Violation of Contract by Landowners at collection of Paddy, 1931 V.S...., Poka 36, Record Section of the Deptt. of Revenue.

suppression of the peasantry, the absence of rights, the bare subsistence conditions, the burden of landowners' interests, and the weak peasant economy all at once led the peasantry to participate in or organize violent movements against the land owning aristocracy. These reasons sometimes led the peasants to take prompt action against their oppressors in the form of physical assault, looting their property, destroying their houses and crops, and sometimes even murder. The traditional type of interrelationships was completely responsible for this type of situation.

The end of the Rana regime and the advent of a democratic system provided the peasantry with the opportunity to speak against age old ruthless exploitation. In fact, they were deprived of the actual benefits of agrarian production. The peasant discontent at that time, however, was combined with the communist ideology. The communists created the very lucrative slogan of "Land to the tiller" to motivate the peasants, and thereby pressured the government to introduce several land laws to bring about changes in the existing land holding and agrarian structures.

* * *

CHAPTER V

THE CHANGING PATTERN OF RELATIONS

In all the agrarian societies, the peasant community always remained as a force to bring about changes in the agrarian system. This chapter deals with peasant activities after 1951. In fact, the increasing of discontent during the Rana rule was related to peasant activities in later years. So, this chapter, which covers the period until 1964 is very important in this context.

As a general rule, the peasantry is systematically disregarded for the most part in social activities in traditional societies, which are dominated by the ruling elite or their subordinates. It is clear that, in country such as Nepal, peasants alone are found to be revolutionary, for they have nothing to loose and everything to gain. The toiling peasantry, through the help of revolutionary leaders, came to know about their real situation and unjust social order. Therefore, they did not hesitate to participate in violent demonstrations against their lords intending ultimately to bring about changes in the existing system and relationship with the landlord. The peasantry as a force also brought about changes in the form of agrarian relations at that time. The peasantry were among those who discovered that only violence pays. For them, there is no compromise, nor possibility of coming to terms. The traditional relations, status of the gentry and protectors of their interests were relatively strong, thereby forming a formidable group against enemies. The peasant community itself constituted a force for change. The change was to occur in the existing pattern of relationships between landlords, intermediaries, local revenue functionaries, peasant cultivators of all kinds, and agristic serfs, or wage labourers in agriculture. The history of middle and working class agitation elsewhere has shown that a large mass of poor peasants impeded the revolution. In fact, in traditional societies, the bulk of the national population is comprised of peasants. In Asian countries where the state controlled all of the land as the ultimate proprietor, the peasant economy remained more traditional and was influenced by the interests of the privileged classes. This was because the state itself handed over its land property rights to individuals. Thereafter, the individual interests of owners, intermediaries etc. compelled to live them under bare subsistence conditions. In Nepal, from the emergence of the Rana regime to the dawn of democracy in 1951, the lack of mechanization in farming and the transformation of the peasant economy led to the continuation of a very backward system of agriculture and land holding. Therefore, during this period, the entire system affected not only other activities of the peasant community, but also the connotation of the term itself. In addition to the popular usage and political connotation of the term, peasant and peasantry have been used to describe a type of rural society and form of economy with reference to regional settings and land tenure. There has been no consistency in the definition due to the varied nature of the peasantry in different tenures. This conceptual inconsistency has had the result that interpretations and analyses of 'peasant society' are by no means comparable in terms of their respective status, rights, economic well being, relationships, subsistence, scope or theoretical underpinnings. The attempts and activities of their leadership mobilized the Nepalese peasantry and encouraged them to speak against the agrarian structure of that time, the exploitation, and their own pitiable condition, which set them apart from other masses of people.[1] This very situation led them to learn about left wing

1. For details in leadership and other movement activities see :
   — Shanker Thapa, 'An Approach to Peasant Movement in Nepal', *Tribhuvan University Journal,* Vo. XIX, June 1996, pp. 74-85

progressive politics and started at the end of the Rana regime. The differences between the Nepalese peasantry and other social or economic groups in the agrarian hierarchy during the pre and post revolution period (1951) in any area or specific to tenure obviously presented difficulties for the former. Such difficulties primarily consisted of economic obligations, rural indebtedness and, to some extent, social status as well.

Therefore, the definition of the term requires consideration of the entire situation. Peasants are those whose ultimate security and subsistence depended upon their having certain land rights, and on the labour of family members. However, they were involved through rights and obligations in a wider economic system which included the privileged groups. The latter were not peasants, but owners. This definition of the Nepalese peasantry reflected the peasants' situations at that time as well as the possible tenurial conditions under which the members of the peasant community cultivated land and fulfilled demands and interests of their lords. The historical fact is that the Nepalese peasantry lived under bare subsistence conditions for centuries. Even until 1951, the peasantry in Nepal did not constitute a force. The entire peasant society was in the form of a fragmented segment, that favoured individual peasants' existence. The network used by the ruling elite to control the entire population of Nepal through different means also created a barrier against the peasant unity. Therefore, there was no organized peasant movement in Nepal before 1951, except for some dissatisfaction which was shown by local peasants in the newly annexed territory of Kumaon against Bam Shah in protest against the exorbitant rates of land tax in comparison to the existing rates which prevailed before the outbreak of the Anglo-Gurkha war in 1814.[2]

But during the political movement against the Ranas during the late 1940's, the Nepalese communists infiltrated and joined forces with the peasants. They also established their base due

2. Ludwig F. Stiller SJ, *The Silent Cry,* Kathmandu : Shahayogi Press, 1976, pp. 301-304.

to the poor conditions of the peasantry and their dissatisfaction provided them with a means of enriching their ideology. For this reason, they supported the peasantry by providing active leadership, and in turn, the peasantry facilitated the acceptance of their ideology to traditional Nepalese society. At the same time, they also made the peasants realize that peasantry itself is a force that might change the entire course of the society. Consequently, the peasantry itself formed a force which was ultimately aimed at changing the existing form of agrarian relations. It has been a very important factor in studying the sociology of Nepalese agriculture and all traditional types of relationships. The peasants' security, subsistence and welfare rested upon the occupancy of a plot for cultivation, but rent payments valuing at least one half of the gross product were beneficial for the cultivators because the rent was regulated at a rate of two-thirds of the gross product excluding all other customary levies. Therefore, their economic and social interests collided with those of the capitalist farmers, feudal lords, landowners and other privileged classes in the agrarian hierarchy. The privileged classes relied solely on what peasants produced. The land had provided owners with economic well being, social dignity, prestige and the basis for their political power. Therefore, the ruling elite placed top priority on obtaining as much land as possible, but they never invested capital in the production process, as a potential means of increasing income, but rather diverted the capital to other sources which were collected through agriculture. In some cases, the local landlords or intermediaries invested limited capital for needy peasants but it was entirely aimed at manipulating of the existing situation in order to accrue benefits from the peasantry, and was not a means of increasing production. Thus, surplus production was never reinvested in the production process.

In this context, it is important to analyze the situation and circumstances under which peasants were placed at the lowest rung of the agrarian hierarchy. It was this placement that created differences with other groups, ultimately causing them to unite as a force against those whose interests collided with those of the peasantry. Therefore, the peasants' socioeconomic status was linked to the process that built the peasantry as a force in Nepal which, by the grace of their power, rebelled against the existing social and agrarian system. In this way, the Nepalese peasantry has been a force for change, but the ideological basis of this phenomenon is obvious.

Before analyzing the peasantry, it is logical to examine various aspects of the situation , such as rent, taxes and levies, cultivation conditions, the peasant economy, peasant dissatisfaction, agitation, pressure for change, the legacy of traditional relationships and promulgation of land laws.

Agrarian Activities and Peasant Discontent:

The system of agrarian taxation before and during the Rana regime favoured the landowners' interests. It was beneficial to them because it guaranteed them higher incomes. The state lost money, but the ruling elite were dominant, owning large areas of land as their *Birtas*. At the same time, the policy of hand over land rights to individuals helped to enlist their support for the regime. The beneficiaries of the existing agrarian system and land holding practices were the ruling elite, nobility and bureaucrats, the regime favoured them at the expense of the peasantry. Therefore, no attempt was made to protect tenants from arbitrary eviction or from exorbitant rent and taxes. During the Rana regime, almost 2/3 of the gross produce was channeled to the landowners in the form of rent, so the rate itself was a burden for the entire peasant community. The peasants' conditions were almost similar on land tenures, such as *Guthi* and *Jagera*, but the conditions of peasants on *Birta* and *Jagir* land was deplorable.

The state relinquished its revenue collection rights to individuals, making them the beneficiaries of state policy under long term settlements. Both such settlements and the regulation of traditional tax rates prevented the state from benefiting economically. So, the Rana regime was prevented from taking advantage of increases in the amount of landowners' property.

They were also authorized to bid on land for cultivation. Therefore, the situation was favourable for evicting cultivators and appointing higher bidders. This was an even greater threat to peasant household economy and subsistence, due to the uncertainty of continued land occupancy. The landowners usually made bids on land for cultivation. The first *Muluki Ain* permitted them to do so.[3] The Birta Taxation Act of 1906 mentioned that rent could be increased only up to the level corresponding to the rates prevailing on adjoining *Raikar* land, but in the Tarai, increases were permitted up to a maximum of ten percent beyond this level. The system of taxation corresponding to adjoining *Raikar* holdings was ambiguous term, and the *Birta* owners took advantages of this ambiguity, especially in places where rent was assessed in kind and collection was made in cash.[4] However, the regime did not impose any restriction on such abuses by individual landowners. The peasants in the hills paid up to 2/3 of the gross produce as rent. In fact, the lack of other means of production led to a higher concentration of the rural population in order to acquire land for cultivation. It was this situation that allowed the landowning elite to impose cultivation terms as they wished and arbitrarily raised the rent. In fact, the amount of rent and methods of its collection played a vital role in determining the fundamental relationship between landlords and peasants. During the Rana regime, this relationship was obviously desirable for the peasants' well being. The most important part of the relationship was that land, as a means of production, was not the property of those who cultivated it.

The tax assessment during the Rana regime was equally variable. The tax rates were exorbitant and oppressive. The

3. *Shri 5 Surendra Vikram Shah ko Palama Baneko Muliki Ain* (The Civil Code Enacted During the Time of King Surendra Bikram Shah), Kathmandu : Ministry of Law and Justice, 2022 V.S. pp. 1-52.
4. M.C. Regmi, *Land Tenure and Taxation in Nepal* (Reprint), Kathmandu : Ratna Pustak Bhandar, 1978, pp. 324-327.

assessment of rent for *Khet* (Paddy fields) and *Pakho* (dry land) varied. The assessment on *Pakho* land was made on the basis of the Haley (ploughed by ox teams) and Bijan (seed) systems. The rates also varied from place to place. The former was fixed on the basis of the ox teams that were used for ploughing whereas the later was fixed on the basis of the seeds that were used for sowing. The Haley system was further divided into *Patey, Kodaley* and *Kutey* holdings,[6] and measured actual areas of land.

The rent for irrigated land was assessed on the basis of the *Adhiya* (Sharecropping) and the *Kut* systems. The former constituted most direct system of rent assessment that had been regulated since the nineteenth century. The owners and cultivators shared total produce in equal proportions on the threshing ground. In fact, the rent was almost one half of gross produce in Khet in the hills. The *Adhiya* system automatically included two other levies *Ghiukhane* and *Chardamtheki* which were payable to the landowners. The *Ghiukhane* levy was paid in lieu of the secondary wheat crop whereas the *Chardamtheki* confirmed the renewal of land occupancy every year. Even in western hill districts, both the *Khet* and *Pakho* lands were cultivated on the basis of *Adhiya*. The cultivators under *Adhiya* were treated as servants, and were evicted even for disobeying the landlords' orders. In principle, the *Mohi* received only the straw and some *Muris* of grain if the harvest was good, and the *Adhiya* system totally ignored the rights of the *Mohi*.[7] At the same time, the landowners had no obligations, nor did they share any of the costs incurred during the production process. This was contrary to the welfare of the sharecroppers, yet it was still better than the *Kut* system. The *Kut* system was practiced in the Kathmandu valley and hill regions. Under that system,

6. Harilal, *Pahad Mal Bishya*, Kathmandu : Nepali Bhasha Prakashini Samiti, 2008 V.S. p. 19.
7. Frank J. Moore (ed.), *Report of the Land Tenure Conditions in Western Nepal*, Kathmandu : Ministry of Land Reforms, 1957, pp. 3-4.

the cultivators were required to pay fixed and stipulated rates of rent. The *Kut* land was assigned to the cultivators through intermediaries; therefore, the interests of the intermediaries were also accommodated for that piece of land. As a result, the cultivators were compelled to satisfy the interests of both. This system required the payment of a fixed amount of rent even in the event of crop failure. So, this situation sometimes resulted in debts for the peasants. The *Birta* owners and *Jagirdars* even used illegal means to collect rent; if peasants could not pay *Kut* to *Jagirdars* in advance or the stipulated rent that was due following crop failures, the absentees or the intermediaries detained them and took all of the grain from their house leaving nothing for them,[8] which resulted in the worst condition for the Nepalese peasantry. Sharecropping was better for the cultivators than the *Kut* system itself, which replaced the former in the second half of the nineteenth century. The exploitation of the peasantry through the exacting of surplus production without increasing total productivity became a symbol of the exploitation of the peasantry by powerful landowners and or by the state.[9] The rates of interest, the rent collection systems and abuses connected there with as well as the ill treatment inflicted by the landowning elite caused hardships and trouble for the peasantry. The existing *Sanads* and *Sawals* were promulgated with the intent of safeguarding the interests of the landowning elite, as the Ranas were more concerned with insuring their fixed and continuous income. The Nepalese peasants' absolute poverty and subsistence level proved to be intolerable, and was responsible for their dissatisfaction. Even though the peasants worked all year round in the fields, they could not retain a sufficient amount of grain. In tenures such as the *Jimidari*, their conditions were the same as those of agristic serfs. A large part of produce was exacted by the *Jimidars* for rent and interest,

8. Padma Bahadur Budhathoki, *Nepalma Kisan Andolan,* Somlingtar : the author, 2045 V.s. pp. 79-98.
9. Peter Dorner, *Land Reforms and Economic Development,* Middlesex : Penguin Books, 1972, p. 131.

and in this case, the peasants would retain only straw,[10] which compelled them to remain in debt forever, with almost no chance of escape. These peasants were also required to pay *Salami, Koshelee* and other customary levies to their masters.

Even in the *Birta* tenure, the owners were entitled to collect non- agricultural taxes and levies. These included *Jhara, Salaami* and *Beth-begar*. These types of taxes provided extra income and privileges to the *Birta* owners, and continued even after the end of the Rana regime. The *Birta* Levies Abolition Act of 1958 ended these traditional practices.[11] The end of the *Birta* system was a historic event and a great relief for the peasants.

The over all agricultural situation before the promulgation of the Land Act of 1964 was most deplorable because of the financial and material responsibilities imposed on the peasantry by the agrarian system and the numerous interests of the privileged classes within the agrarian hierarchical structure.

The agricultural situation in Nepal even after the end of the Ranas' autocracy was not favourable for good agriculture. The 1950s, of course, marked the beginning of reforms through legal promulgation. The situation fostered dissatisfaction and discontent among the peasant cultivators, who demanded total changes in the agrarian system.

Cultivation Conditions and Tenurial Situation:

The land holding and tenurial conditions in Nepal during the Rana regime gave rise to different types of land problems. A vast areas of land was owned by a small number of big landlords, but they neither managed nor cultivated the land, they only rented land for cultivation. The separation of land

---

10. Louis J. Wallinsky, *Selected Papers of Wolf Ladjinsky : Agrarian Reforms as an Unfinished Business,* New York : Oxford University Press, 1977, pp. 316-323.
11. *Birtawarley Birtama Rakam Lagai Linakhana Napauney Ain 2015* (Birta Levies Abolition Act 1958), *Nepal Gazette,* Pt. VIII, No. 19 (Extraordinary), 18 Marga, 2015 V.S. Section 3a and 3b.

ownership and cultivation strongly affected farms' output.

The tenurial conditions and status of cultivators in tenures such as the Raikar, Birta, Jagir, Guthi, Kipat, Rakam, and Ukhada were similar, and represented the worst and most exploitative tenurial conditions. They were subject to numerous taxes, levies etc, but cultivated the land with almost no rights on the particular piece of land that they cultivated.

The *Birta* owners and the *Jagirdars* were the absentee landlords, and obtained property and proprietary land rights. The intermediaries remained in between in order to manage land on behalf of the absentees. Cultivators were hired to cultivate land, so the lack of employment opportunities in rural areas led to a higher concentration of the rural population on that land.

The rights of *Birta* owners were not limited to the collection of rent and levies, but included as many as thirty-six types of taxes (36 *Kara*) including customs duties, forest revenue, pasture tax, hemptax, market tax, judicial fines, escheat property, a monopoly on export duties, on hides and skins, liquor taxes, and judicial and police power.[12] Other people besides the peasants were also require to pay several taxes, but the rights of Birta owners and intermediaries mainly affected the *Birta* cultivators. Therefore, these rights were beneficial only for the recipients and not for the actual cultivators, and the owners had no tax liabilities. Finally people demanded the abolition of the *Birta* tenure.[13]

The ruling elite, the *Rajautas*, nobility, bureaucracy, absentees, local moneylenders, resident landowners, intermediaries, local revenue functionaries all contributed to the oppression of the peasantry, as did the agrarian relations of that time. All possible rights were vested in the landowners, who were the recipients of specific land grants. As for the peasants, however, alternative sources of income were hardly

12. Regmi, f.n. 4, p. 256.
13. Basupasa, *Pharkera Herdṣa,* (looking behind) Kathmandu : Pasa Prakashan, 2044 V.S. pp. 93-96.

available to them, so their status, and lack of rights, combined with the powers and prerogatives of the landlords, the state's bias in favour of the highest level of the structural hierarchy, and the role and responsibilities of the intermediaries contributed to the former's exploitation and suppression. The most powerful level of the agrarian society actually lived luxurious lives at the expense of the impoverished peasants, who cultivated regardless of the conditions imposed on them by the owners. Although, they were dissatisfied with the existing system none of them were in a position to speak against it. They were also deprived of adequate means of production. Although, they were treated as tools of production. The lack of monetization, higher rate of rural indebtedness, lack of adequate means of production, the privileges of the higher stratum, interests of the rulers, and higher concentration of the rural population in agriculture all adversely affected the cultivators. The peasants were born in fields, grew up with spade, and died in the fields with almost nothing to show for it. This was generally the fate of all the cultivators. This kind of problem led to economic under-development and backwardness.[14]

A large number of land problems originated during the Rana regime. The peasant cultivators suffered from a large number of such problems, which had far reaching consequences for the peasant economy as well as in the future course of their activities, such as—

— The absence of cultivators' rights on the land which they cultivated.
— Tenurial insecurity,
— The existence of Intermediaries, mostly in tax exempt tenures.
— Growing rural landlessness and lack of adequate means of production.
— High rates of rent, taxes and levies

14. Atiur Rahman, *Peasant and Classes : A Study of Differentiationin Bhangladesh,* Delhi : Vikas Publishing House, 1986, p. VIII.

Due to the land problems, the peasant economy in Rana Nepal was very weak. The landowning elite and rich peasants constituted only 10% of the total national population, but they controlled almost 60% of the total cultivable land. Altogether, 65 % of the population didn't have sufficient land.[15]

2. The Generation of Peasant Discontent :

The overall situation led to increasing peasant discontent, which finally caused changes in the nature of the traditional society. The peasants' activities developed independently of other non-professional movements. The activities of the peasant class and extremist leadership influenced their revolutionary strategy. The peasantry had always been the major force in conflict with the landlords and their subordinates. In such cases, the peasants and the landless rural agricultural serfs had no fear of loosing anything. Many of them literally owned neither a tile over their heads nor a speck of land under their feet, but they were the backbone of peasant associations, the vanguard in the overthrow of the feudal forces, and the heroes who performed the great revolutionary tasks which for long years were left undone.[16]

The conditions of the peasantry in Nepal was not satisfactory, so, they were not satisfied with their conditions. They were illiterate but they were not ignorant, and no analysis of agrarian relations or the status of the peasantry is complete without analyzing indicators of living and working conditions and the role played by the landowners and intermediaries in a broader perspective.

The agrarian system did not witness any major changes until 1964. The regime was concerned only with the collection of rent and taxes and with protecting the interests of the

15. Keshab Badal, *Kisanko Kitab* (The Book of Peasants), Kathmandu : Pairavi Prakashan, 2047 V.S., pp. 4-5.
16. Mao-tse Tung, "Report on an Investigation of the Peasant Movements in Human", in *Selected Works of Maotse Tung,* Vol. 1, Peking : Foreign Language Press, 1967, pp. 32-33.

landowning elite, so, the peasants remained secondary in this aspect and were hardly given any importance even though they continued to be the principal force in the production process. In reality, the Nepalese peasants suffered from all of the disadvantages found in the poorest rural areas throughout Asia, including marginal fragmented holdings and keen competition for land.[17] Furthermore, the cultivating community was completely subject to the will of the landlords, which made it necessary for them to obtain the landlords guarantee that they would be able to remain on the land. Also in spite of their investment of labour and capital into production without any outside aid, they had no means of procuring their rightful share of the agrarian produce. Nonetheless, they paid up to 2/3 of the gross crop as rent, excluding other payments. In the Western and Eastern Tarai where the Jimidari system prevailed, the peasant cultivators were reduced to one basic meal a day or even less if they did not have additional income.[18] They remained in this state for centuries, without any significant changes in their status. Traditionally, the agents of the state and favourites of the ruling elite were to be granted land as a reward and either subjected to nominal taxes or none at all. In this way, they became the owners of vast areas of land. The transfer of land ownership rights not only determined their control over a certain area of land, but also over the inhabitants residing in the area. However, the transfer of rights by the state was not absolute.

The Rana rulers appointed *Talukdars, Mukhiya, Mulmi, Jimmawal* and others to collect revenue, as well as *Zamindars*, who collected revenue on behalf of the regime and retained 5% to 10% of total collection. They also maintained all records pertaining to the land. As a rule, they exploited people, captured fertile land by unjust means, took bribes, and punished peasants without appropriate reasons in order to maintain their

17. Wallinsky, f.n. 10, p. 317.
18. Geofrey C. Gunn, *Rebellion in Laos : Peasants in a Colonial Backwater*, Boulder : West View press, 1990, p. 76.

dominance. They also exacted *beth-begar*. All the extra legal payments were the burden for peasants, and compelled to live in bare subsistence conditions.[19] The impact of the *Kamaiya* system including *Hali* and *Harwa* etc. were the worst of the land holding system at that time.[20] The Rana rulers did not understand that land ownership reforms had a direct impact on production which would lead to the improvement of the national economy. The tenants-at-will, sharecropping and fixed rate tenancies were the worst forms that were practiced. In places, where rent was fixed at standard rates, especially in the Kathmandu valley and central hills, rent collection was facilitated without sharing the actual produce at the threshing ground. This provided to the Jagirdars and Birta owners with fixed income status.[21] The *Birta* owners however, usually rented land for cultivation to higher bidders in order to maximize their share of the agrarian product.

Another problem in terms of the peasants' land rights was the fact that their land rights were not well defined due to the lack of records describing it. The Ranas in general did not improve these conditions, and it was not until six years after the end of Rana regime that a new code fixed rent at the rate of one half of the gross produce. Nonetheless, even until 1964, a tenant paid from one *muri* to one *muri* ten *pathis* of semi milled rice and 5 *pathis* to one *muri* ten *pathis* of wheat per *Ropani* of land to individual landowners, which was defined as *Kut*. In addition to this, the peasants were required to donate hay, red soil, white soil, straw mats, barley etc. as gifts in the Kathamdnu valley. Similarly, free labour was also provided during ceremonies, times of illness, child rearing, festivals, and rituals. The landowners enjoyed extensive rights over cultivators. The

---

19. *The Manifesto of the Akhil Nepal Kisan Sangh and its policies*, Kathmandu : ANKS, 2047 V.S., p. 19.
20. *Nepalma Kamaiya Pratha Bhitra Bandha Majdoor* (Bonded Labour Within the Kamaiya System in Nepal), Kathmandu : INSEC, 2049, V.S., pp. 37-85.
21. Stiller, f.n. 2, p. 59.

wages of agrarian labourers in 1951 was 1.2 *anas* to 4 *anas* a day. The *Jagir Guthi* and *Rakam* tenures were considered as burden for them.[22] The *Guthi* rent was fixed at the rate of 37 *pathis* and 4 manas of rice per *Ropani*, but the registered tenants collected 40 to 55 *pathis* from cultivating tenants. The situation was so bad that after 1951, the Nepali Congress was also compelled to raise its voice for changes in the traditional type of agrarian system. Therefore, in 1951, the Congress proposed the following points in order to bring about changes in agriculture.

— to abolish Birta to solve other related problems,
— to put to an end to the Raja Rajautas, and
— to abolish the Beth-begari and Jhara systems, which were still oppressive for the peasants.

The leaders did not support revolutionary changes in land holding practices under the pretext that it was not the proper time for it.[23] The reformist politicians believed that an attempt to secure tenancy rights was sufficient whereas, the revolutionaries wanted to transfer ownership rights to the peasants and to make the slogan of -"Land to the tiller" a reality.[24] Thus, a reform movement required in order to save peasants from maltreatment and exploitation by the landed aristocracy. However, even the political changes of 1951 could not bring about changes in the existing form of agrarian relations, so, the situation continued as before. The peasants felt it necessary to unite and organize a movement for a better future, but until 1952, the government of Nepal realized for the first time in

22. Krishna Bhakta Chaguthi, *Kisanko Abastha* (The Conditions of Peasants), Bhaktapur : The Author, n.d., pp. 5-14.
23. *Nepali Congress le Kisanharu ko Lagike Garyo?* (What Has Nepali Congress Done For Peasants?) Kathmandu, Nepali Congress, n.d., p. 2.
24. Bhagwan Ratna Tuladhar, "Nepalko Rajnaitik Vikasama Kisan Andolam ko Bhumika" (The Role of Pesant Movements in the Political Development of Nepal)", *Jhilko,* Year 10, No. 2, Kathmajdu : Ashwin 2046, V.S., p. 36.

history that there were acute land problems and formed committees to investigate the problems and find ways to liberate the peasantry. The major achievement of this attempt was that the committees primarily suggested—

— To free the peasants from debt, and
— To form a mobile court to protect peasant cultivators from oppression by feudal lords.

However, no changes were introduced, so, the situation remained intact. Therefore, the peasantry began to mobilize their forces against traditionalism. The forms of resistance ran the gamut from rent evasion to armed revolt to class struggle and to aggression against their enemies. Such activities might have taken a more prosaic form. J. C. Scott has termed it- "the every day form of peasant resistance." The prosaic form of struggle was a constant struggle between the peasantry and those who exacted labour and interest from them through foot dragging, dissimulation, desertion, pilfering, slander and so forth.[25] The mobilization of peasant forces and their dissatisfaction with the traditional practices took multiple forms in response to the regional conditions and the degree of economic and political coercion that existed everywhere.[26] The peasant-cultivators in the Limbuwan area for instance, put forward various demands relating to *Kipat* holdings, agrarian conditions and debt contracts. Later on, political ideology also entered into their way of thinking, which greatly influenced the peasants and also took various forms.[27]

The conditions of the peasantry was very precarious until the 1950s. Obviously, the Land Reform Act of 1964 brought about perceptible changes in the existing land holding system in Nepal, but it too could not bring about complete reforms in

25. J.C. Scott, *Weapons of the Weak : Everyday Form of Pesant Resistance,* New Heaven : Yale University Press, 1985, p. - XIV.
26. Gunn, f.n. 18, p. 101.
27. B.B. Chemjong, *Pallokirat Limbuwanka Maghru* (Demands of Pallokirat Limbuwan), Asan, Nepal Press, 2014 V.S., pp. 3-5 and 7.17.

agriculture. Some of the defective tenurial practices remained intact, and even if we considered the last quarter of this century, the situation seems to be very bad. The practice of sharecropping or *Bataiya* has been a common practice both in the hills and the *Tarai*.

Land problems have constituted the most important problems in Nepal, and must be considered to be a priority. The problems at the end of the Rana regime led to the formulation of the Tenancy Rights Acquisition Act of 2008 V.S., which was formulated to help the toiling peasantry. At that time, tenancy rights and the *Kut* systems were the two main factors which sparked the confrontation between landlords and tenant cultivators. The latter were led by middle class activists, and the clashes finally resulted in the promulgation of the Act.

The Nepalese peasants, under the leadership of *Akhil Nepal Kisan Sangh,* strongly demanded the implementation of the act, which collided with the interests of the Nepalese gentry, who demanded its repeal. The rulers of Nepal had never favoured the cultivating classes, so they repealed the Act under the pretext of the lack of cultivators' records.[28] Consequently, there were many of peasant movements right after 1951 which were in fact, the result of old practices which prevailed at the end of the Rana's rule.

The land commissions in the Tarai investigated various problems and suggested ways to cope with them. The commissions suggested the following changes—

- The cultivators registered in 2007 V.S. had to be allowed to continue to occupancy land as cultivators, so, evictions had to be restricted at all levels.
- The *Bataiya* rate of 3 or 4 *kur* which had been in effect until that time would be allowed to continue.
- All debt bonds required investigation to determine their authenticity. Therefore, the *Zamindars* would not be allowed to deduct part of their loans for the crop of the

28. *Manifesto of Ahkil Nepal Kisan Sangh (ANKS) and its Policies,*

following year, and

— The *Badahakims* (district governors) would be ordered to stop all kinds of evictions before the mobile court made any decision.

Agrarian Conditions in The Tarai and Hills :

In the Western Tarai, a tax was levied and regulated on land which had been surveyed and duly registered in revenue cadasters. However, the *Zamindars* collected *Bataiya* even from that land, so, it was demanded that such land had to be registered in the names of the actual cultivators. The *Zamindars* were the most powerful of the landowners. In Kailali alone, they registered 5120 *bighas* in the names of their relatives, so, this land was demanded by the cultivators. The former agreed to return 2173 after 1951. 13,870 *bighas* of surplus land was kept in the names of the Raitis (ordinary people) but was controlled by the *Zamindars*, who exacted all produce from it. Therefore, the actual cultivators had to be identified in order to confirm their rights. Actually, almost 22,000 *bighas* of land belonged to cultivating tenants in Kailali, but all of the earnings were taken by the *Zamindars*. Thus, all of the peasants intended to stop such practices immediately and initiate proper settlements during the 2007 V.S. survey. The cultivators also intended to reclaim land within the areas where the *Zamindars* prevented them from doing so, but the situation in Kailali itself was worse at the end of 1951.

In the Butwal area where the *Ukhada* tenure prevailed, the situation was worst. During the survey of 1952 V.S. almost 75% to 80% of the total cultivated land belonged to the cultivators, but the exploitative activities of the *Zamindars* and *Patuwaris* had reversed this situation.[29] It further waned during the survey of 1979 V.S. mainly because the rich landlords, by virtue of their ability, status and cunning, seized such land through investment under the pretext of exchanging land. During the *Ukhada* investigation, a certain areas of land was

29. Nepali Congressley ... f.n. 23, p. 22.

recorded as the *Ukhada* category A.[30] These peasants also demanded that they should get back their land as recorded in the survey of 1952 V.S., but the *Zamindars* claimed that the ownership rights of such land belonged to them.[31] The situation worsened to the extent that Prime Minister Padma Shumsher despatched an Ukhada investigation committee in 2004 V.S..[32] Later, at the end of the Rana's rule, it was revealed that the cultivators hardly occupied ¼ of the areas, whereas ½ of the total areas fell under the control of the landlords. The *Zamindars* continued their demands, settled *Raitis* for cultivation, and registered land in their own names. The peasants in the Butwal area cultivated land of different categories which included—

- Own *Mal* Land *(Tirja or Numbari)*
- Zamindari *Seer*
- Land registered on *Ukhada* form A', and
- *Marta Parta* or Surplus land that was not registered in the name of the *Zamindars*, but from which they collected rent.

The practice of *Bataiya* was not favourable for tenants in the Butwal area. Usually, the area cultivated by a peasant was less than that mentioned in the survey field map. Even in spite of this, they had to pay Kut on the basis of such papers. Thus, they paid rent for larger areas than they cultivated. There was no incentive for cultivators to improve the land. The manipulation of survey records to change the exact boundaries of the plot was also one of the means of exploiting peasant cultivators. The landlords also consolidated fragmented holdings into bigger plots, which were comprised of the most productive land. The tenant cultivators therefore did not even know which particular plot they were supposed to occupy.

30. The land obtained by cultivators form landlords was called *Ukahda* category A land.
31. Nepali Congress..., f.n. 23,pp. 22-23.
32. Balchandra Sharma, *Nepalko Aitihasik Ruprekha* (Historical Outline of Nepal), Benaras : K.K. Devi, 2022 V.S., p. 368.

When they realized that they had been cultivating smaller plots than were mentioned in the records, they wished to pay rent which corresponded to the actual area of cultivation. This finally led to a confrontation with the *Zamindars*, who did not accept their demands. On the other hand, the *Zamindars* also claimed that newly reclaimed land should not be given to peasants because they had incurred all of the expenses necessary to reclaim it. The small size *Zamindars* also raised their voices, claiming that they had only 9 to 10 *bighas* of Seer land which was cultivated by tenants, and that they feared loosing all of their property if it was given to tenant cultivators.

The *Zamindars* and *Patuwaris* controlled peasants in different ways. The latter were not only required to fulfill interests of the former, but they were also moved from one place to another, so, they were unable to hold land permanently under these conditions. Even forests, ponds and lakes were registered in the names of landlords which further frustrated the peasants.

The Butwal Land Commission of 1951 also gave various suggestions regarding land holding and tenurial conditions.

- To register land in the name of the cultivators.
- To prohibit the exacting of excessive Kut for Ukhada land.
- To prohibit landlords from seizing the peasants' land.
- To form a committee of peasants to fight against any kind of abuse by the landlords.
- To collect and maintain statistics in order to find out about the seizeure of land from peasants by the landlords through unjust means.
- To form a mobile court to settle disputes between landlords and peasants, and
- To establish agricultural laboratories and a branch for animal husbandry to help peasants.

In Bardia also, the land problem was considered to be serious. The Kamaiya system was prevalent, and reduced peasants to the status of agrarian serfs. Thus, the situation in

Bardia was worse than in any other district in the western Tarai. This situation continued even after 1951. So, the peasants demanded the dispatch of a committee to Bardiya to investigate the problem.

Finally, it was decided—[33]

— To distribute 14,000 bighas of second grade Seer land.
— To abolish all kinds of unauthorized taxes and levies.
— To restrict and prohibit *Zamindars* from collecting *Bataiya* from land registered in the names of cultivators, and
— To investigate problems in the existing agrarian relationships.

The survey of 2004 V.S. in Bardia revealed a number of land problems. The survey map itself was full of errors. The changes in boundaries created further clashes. The cultivators claimed their rights on particular plots, on which they withheld rent payments. The landowners in Bardia and other districts also exacted excessive rent, and the cultivating peasants were ignorant of their actual plots. The Bardia Commission then regulated the Bataiya rent. The cultivators demanded 5 Kur Bataiya on Seer land and compensation for excessive rent. Finally, 4 Kur Bataiya was fixed. This decision ended the preliminary clash between them. At that time, the clashes over Bataiya rates created discontent to the extent that the Zamindars dumped all of the grain on the threshing ground without giving the peasants their share. This left the peasants in a state of starvation, but they were still ready to struggle for their rights. However, the rights of the landowners and their economic well being remained the dominant factor in the existing form of agrarian relations, and led to further changes in the existing pattern of land ownership. The figures below are significant in describing the Zamindars' domination and the helplessness of the peasantry.[34]

---

33. Nepali Congress ....., f.n. 23, pp. 10-11.
34. *Ibid*, p. 19, Also See : Regmi, f.n. 5, p. 117

Table No: 3
Changes in Land ownership in Bardia

Years	Bighas 1910	Bighas 1951
Individual Owners	52000	24000
Jimidars	24000	52000

The land survey of 2004 V.S. did not take into account the law or practices of that time. The survey team settled land problems only on the basis of existing documentary evidences, which had been produced by the *Zamindars* and *Patwaris*, and did not examine the old records in which the land belonging to the peasants, landlords and his relatives were registered. Consequently, the land of peasants was registered in the name of the landlords, thus, the *numbari* land of peasants was handed over to landlords, depriving them of land rights which they had held since 1867 V.S. Similarly, the land which had been reclaimed by peasants was also registered in the name of the landlords. This not only fueled the peasants' anger toward the landlords, but also turned them against the survey teams. The land types listed below were occupied by the landlords through unjust means.[35]

— The registered numbari land of peasants which was determined during the survey of 1967 V.S.

— Land registered in the name of fake cultivators in order to prolong land ownership by landlords. This type of land formerly belonged to cultivating tenants, and was registered as uncultivated or barren in order to escape all kinds of controversies relating to occupancy or ownership rights, and

— The owners forced peasants to contract loans and persuaded them to reclaim land. When they defaulted on loan repayments, the plot was mortgaged as collateral and went up for auction. The *Zamindars* purchased it in the name of their servants for low prices.

35. Nepali Congressley..., f.n. 23, pp. 13-14.

In this situation, they acted like medieval feudal and autocratic rulers. All of these situations compelled the government to reconsider the existing land problem. Consequently, the government decided -

- to return all land to the cultivators which was forcefully occupied by the big landlords.
- to set up a special tribunal to investigate how the peasants lost the land that they had cultivated for many years.
- to provide 7 days time to submit evidence in order to claim rights.
- to inform peasants about it prior to the arrival of the special tribunal in the districts, and
- the tribunal had to investigate upon all requests received from peasants.

The commission investigated landlord-tenant relations and suggested ways for landlords to avoid using unjust means of exploiting the tenants.[36] The investigation originally decided that all debts should be contracted only on government stamped paper, three witnesses from village *Panchayats* (local administrative units) were be required, and the peasants had to be issued receipts upon payment of rent.

At that time, it was necessary for the government to act on behalf of the peasants, but even the Bardia Commission was unable to help peasants because the land owning community was still more powerful in all land related matters, and influenced the commission's personnel. Finally, the commission recommended—

- The *Bataiya* exacted from peasants on numbari land from 1947 to 1951 should be used to reduce the debt extended to them by the *Zamindars*. They had exacted excessive levies and taxes and therefore had to be punished accordingly.
- The peasants were required to work Seer land (*Sail Seer*) without wages, and were compelled to contract loans

36. *Ibid.*, pp. 15-17.

for subsistence too. The *Zamindars* who forced them to do this were to be punished accordingly.

— In 1967 V.S., Numbari and Seer land encompassed 52,000 and 24,000 bighas respectively, but this situation had been reversed by 2008 V.S. Therefore, the ratio of *Zamindari* Seer was not to exceed 30% on *Mauja* of 100 bigha, 60% for 100 to 300 bighas, and 15% percent for *Mauja* of more than 300 *bighas*. All excess Seer land was to be given to the cultivators.

— The debt bonds that were forcefully contracted in lieu of grain which had been looted by the peasants during the movement of 2007 V.S. had to be canceled because the peasants were not able to return it.

— The loans extended by moneylenders were extra financial burden for the peasants, so, all unjust bonds had to be canceled because peasants could not extricate themselves from the burden of debt. Appropriate bonds could be entertained, but the moneylenders were ordered to collect it in five installments.

— The worst forms of tenancy, the traditional type of agrarian relations in Bardia, and the role of the regime in protecting all of the interests of the landed aristocracy eventually forced 75% of the total population to remain *Kamaiyas*. Therefore, all the *Martaparta* and other excess land had to be given to them sothat they would not remain entirely dependent on landlords in order to obtain land for cultivation or forced to fulfill their every demand. - It was also necessary to set up village councils and schools for the *Kamaiyas*' welfare, and

— Assist farmers and provide incentives for land reclamation.

The commission, however, submitted the report to the government, but it was not faithfully implemented. It is very important to know about the feudal nature of Nepalese society in this regard. The landed aristocracy and Birta owning Ranas played a vital role in Nepalese politics. Even after 1951, the

Nepali Congress was not capable of opposing the interests of the land owning aristocracy, because the party itself was comprised of the landowning elite and big landlords. Thus, the situation was not likely to end the remnants of medieval feudalism. Nepal lacked revolutionary legal enactment to introduce reforms in existing land holding practices. B.P. Koirala also favoured the peasant community in his speeches during that time, but he, too, could not do anything to improve their conditions to the extent that the peasants desired. Even after the political changes in 1951, the situation remained as before, so, all other efforts became useless. This situation also led the peasantry to participate in movements.

The conditions of peasantry in the entire western Tarai were unsatisfactory. Their conditions was similar to their counterparts in other parets of the country.[37] The *Kamaiya* system was the result of traditional types of agrarian relationships. In that region, 82% of the total area was cultivated by the Tharu farmers.[38] The pattern of land holding in the western Tarai changed gradually since the survey of 1967 V.S.. If we look at the case in Bardia only, it makes the entire picture clear. During the survey in 1967 V.S., almost 81,000 bighas were cultivated of which 54,000 *bighas* were Raitan (numbari) and 21,000 bighas were *Zamindari* Seer. But in 37 years, in 2004 V.S., these statistics changed to 31,432 *bighas* and 42,088 *bighas* respectively. In 15 more years, it further changed to 30,911 and 51,973 bighas respectively.[39] This data clearly shows that Raitan land was gradually taken by the landowning community and converted into *Zamindari Seer*. In this way, peasant cultivators lost their own land. This system worsened the

37. K.P. Srivastav, *Nepal ki Kahani* (The Story Districts and Land Reform), New Delhi : Atma Ram and Sons, 1955, pp. 112-124.
38. HMG, *Sora Jilla ra Bhumi Sudhar* (Sixteen Districts and Land Reforms), Kathmandu : department of Land Reforms, 2024 V.S., pp. 189-190.
39. Badri Prasad Pahadi, *Bardia Jillama Bhumisudhar* (Land Reform in Bardia Districts), Kathmandu : Department of Land Reforms, 2023 V.S., p. 5.

conditions of the peasantry and further complicated land problems.

As for the debt situation, in a few cases, the Rana rulers ordered the creditors to wait for a longtime before collecting loans,[40] but the debtors were required to pay *Salaami* in the form of Ghee, fuel wood, beth-begar, vegetables, fruits, red soil, service, and so forth.

The *Thari, Mukhiya, Talukdar, Jimidars*, and other functionaries also exploited peasants using unjust means. In villages, the landlords and their associates remained very powerful and influential.

As the consequence of this, the rich landlords in villages asked peasants to sign certain papers. They lied that the papers were related to rent payment, but in fact, such papers were manipulated and converted into *Rajinamah*, which indicated voluntary relinquishment of land rights.

Tenancy was unregulated, as was rent on a standard level. The peasants were evicted frequently, and therefore, could not give proper attention to their production activities.

From 1951 to 1959, there were a large number of peasant movements. During this time, the exploited peasants organized themselves against the landlords in order to change oppressive and unacceptable practices.[41] The professional peasant uprisings were gradually influenced by political ideology, and after 1960, the banned political parties found favourable ground with which to foster their activities in the peasant movements. Along with political interests, they addressed various land issues and other related problems. The major problems, among others were the *Kut*, levies and tenancy rights. The peasants paid up to 70% Of the paddy's production for rent and taxes.[42] In fact, this rate

40. Royal order to the creditors of Hari Datta Padhya, 1866 V.S., *Regmi Research Series* 14 : 17, July 1982, p. 105. 1866 V.S.
 — Royal Order on Debt of Ram Deomjhi-1882 V.S. *Regmi Research Series.*
41. Mohan Bikram Singh, "Bhadra 24 ka Andolan (The Movement of Bhadra 24th.)", *Jhilko,* 10:2, 2046 V.S. pp. 91-7.
42. Regmi, f.n. 4, p. 105.

was higher than the rate paid by their counterparts in India.[43] Sometimes, the peasants were denied the chance to cultivate because they could not pay the proscribed rent and taxes. In many cases, they even deserted villages in order to move to other places.

In general, the high rates of rent and taxes, the inavailability of justice, dominance, and dependency all combined to complicate agrarian relations, and it was the very situation that provided a favourable ground for mass dissatisfaction and for organizing movements of a different nature. Various land laws were promulgated after the end of the Rana regime. Of course, such laws introduced certain changes in the agrarian system, but they too, could not bring about the desired changes. All of the laws were inadequate in the context of agrarian reforms. Therefore, an independent Land Reforms Commission was also formed to deal with the problem. The lack of peasants' rights records ruined the peasant economy and proved to be an obstacle to economic development in all ages.[44]

The rent composition, conditions of cultivation, landowners' rights, absentees, intermediaries and cultivators, status and position of village moneylenders in the rural societies, rates of interest, nature of land mortgages, and the household economy of peasant cultivators are directly related to the nature of the existing agrarian relations in Nepal. Of course, the peasant cultivators played a vital role in agricultural production activities, but their position was at the lowest rung of the agrarian hierarchy. They could not get adequate land rights during the Rana regime, and their role in the production process was neither appreciated by the state nor by the landowners themselves. Economic factors, which forced the peasants to work in the fields even under the most unfavourable conditions, and their relations with the land owning elite were based on financial terms rather than socio-cultural factors.

43. Stiller, f.n. 2, p. 298.
44. UNO, *Land Reforms : Defects in Agrarian Structure on Obstacle to Economic Development,* New York : U.N. Department of Economic Affaris, 1951, p. 17.

The *Muluki* Ain and other Sawals discussed different aspects of the agricultural system, but sometimes, even they could not stop landowners, absentees, or intermediaries from taking illegal activities against the cultivators. Even in Kathmandu valley, conditions for the peasantry were unsatisfactory. The *Guthi* rent was comparatively higher for the peasants, and in some places, including some parts of Kathmandu valley, the *Guthi* rent did not correspond to the rates prescribed for adjoining *Raikar* holdings. It was fixed at the rate of 37.4 *Pathis* of rice per *Ropani* of land, the peasants cultivating Guthi land had a chance to retain just a little grain after the payment of rent and levies. On the contrary, the intermediary tenants could keep 2 *Pathis* 4 *Manas* to 17 *Pathis* 4 *Manas* of rice as their share, but there was no chance of reducing the rent. Protest movements and demonstrations were organized in all areas of the Kathmandu valley, which compelled the government to declare a 13 point reforms plan. The movement itself was a major step against exploitative payments. During this movement, the peasant activists complained and stopped other peasants from carrying sacks of rice to pay as rent to the Guthi institution or to the *Birta* owners.[45] Consequently, in 1953 *Guthi*, rent was reduced to 1 *Muri* 5 *Pathi* in which one-third of gross produce was payable in cash at the rate of Rs. 6.0 per *Muri* of rice. At that time, it was considered to be a relief to the peasant community, but levies such as Rakams such as *Beth-begar*, *Sauney fagu* and *Ghiukhaney* etc. were also payable in cash. The rates of *Sauneyfagu* were Rs. 0.07 to 0.14.[46] The cultivators invested labour and, seeds and performed manuring in order to produce grain. In Kathmandu valley and its periphery, 2 to 4 *Muris* of rice were produced on first grade *Abal* land. The landowners at the end of the Rana rule were not very friendly towards tenants. The land owners had the right to detain peasants in their houses if they failed to pay rent. Thus, organizations such as -the *Kirshi Sudhar Sangh, Akhil Nepal Kishn Sangh* and *Akhil Nepal*

45. Chauguthi, f.n. 22, pp. 5-15.
46. Budhathoki, f.n. 8. pp. 1-3.

Suddhikaran Kisan Sangh favoured agricultural changes. They insisted that[47]

— Land ownership belongs to the government. So, land taxes should be paid only to the government not to individuals, and

— Land must belong to those who cultivate it.

The movements since 1951 were basically concerned with rent, peasant's rights, land distribution, and the abolition of levies. The leaders further demanded the abolition of feudal and semi-feudal elements from the land.[48] The Land Reforms Commissions also agreed upon and approved 6 popular demands of the *Suddhikaran Kisan Sangh*, but the suppression of peasants continued, along with the traditional agricultural exploitation. In 1952, the government planned to the suppress movements and sent a '*Rakshya Dal* Contingent' to Somlingtar (Bhaktapur) where the central office of the *Suddhikarn Kisan Sangh* was functioning. This activity benefited the peasants by changing the price rate for rice, which was fixed at the rate of Rs. 8.0 to 13.0 per *Muri*. In 1954, the government agreed to extend the time limit for rent payments reduce rice payments to amounts payable at government rates, and change the payment of *Guthi* rent to one half in cash and the other half in kind. Similarly, the rent rate on adjoining *Raikar* and *Guthi* tenures in the Kathmandu valley was also declared uniform wherever it varied, but this agreement was not properly implemented. Therefore, the peasant leaders put forward more demands and demonstrated against the government, but the government arrested its leaders in order to suppress the movement.[49] The goal of the professional peasant organizations was the improvement of the Nepalese cultivators' conditions.[50]

---

47. *Manifesto of the All Nepal Peasants Purification Association,* Somlingtar, Publicity Department, 2007, pp. 1-6.
48. *Pamphlet of the ANPPA* 2011 V.S.
49. Budhathoki, f.n. 8, pp. 30-34.
50. Pasa, f.n. 13, pp. 93-96.

So, various movements were organized against unjust practices. The Nepali Congress also worked for the peasant community in order to improve their conditions.[51]

The movement largely benefited the peasant community in the country. The Kirtipur movement of the *Suddhikaran Kisan Sangh* compelled the government to promulgate an act which agreed to pay compensation to the tenants, while it acquired land. Until 1960, peasants were permitted to transfer tenancy rights through registration procedures but this was suspended thereafter. Thus, they became merely an economic unit to till land and pay rent. The Land Reforms Act of 1964 also empowered the land owners to evict tenants on charges of refusing to make payments or for making homestead sites. During the Rana's rule, a tenant could be evicted if he did not pay rent for three consecutive years. But after 1964, the time limit was reduced to one year. Most of the peasants regarded it as an additional form of extra exploitation and suppression of the community.

The new rate granted relief to the peasants cultivators. In 1964 a new survey of land was conducted in different districts. It fixed exact areas of land and rent was fixed accordingly. The old system of rent assessment was abandoned and a new act was enforced, it also could not satisfy the peasant community. They began to demand that tenancy right should be made salable, transferable and divisible among the heirs of the *Mohi* in order to guarantee more benefits.[52] During the Rana regime, the lack of proper legislation for the regulation of land measurements led to the manipulation of the land area by the owners, so sometimes the cultivators paid *Kut* for considerably larger areas than the actual cultivated area. The peasant leaders in Nepal organized meaningful peasant movements, particularly in the Tarai districts, against exploitative landlords and moneylenders. A large number of people were involved in such

---

51. R.B. Jyapu, *Nepal Ma Kisan Andolan* (Peasant Movement in Nepal), Kathmandu : Yuba Sahitya Gosthi, n.d., pp. 1-18.
52. Chauguthi, f.n. 22, p. 30.

movements, which addressed the issues of rates of rent, tenancy rights, the eviction of tenants, opposition to the compulsory saving scheme, starvation, maltreatment by the landlords, exploitation etc. These conflicts were between landlords and tenants, police and villagers, landlords and villagers, the state and peasants, and so on. Three-fourths of the cases occurred in the Tarai in the 1950s, which was due to the fact that it had the highest concentration of tenants in the region.

The rural production system in Nepal entailed many hard ships, none of which were suffered by the landowners, even though they expected to collect all of the rent due. In the Kut system, payment waivers were not granted, even if the production was not adequate or the crops failed.

The agrarian system that prevailed during the Rana regime needed reforms in order to make it confirm to modern realities. The system continued even after the Land Reforms Commission (1962) proposed to introduce reforms.[53] The land records clearly distinguished between registered tenants and cultivators. This distinction has contributed to exploitation by intermediaries and middlemen and the registered tenants and land owners were categorized as such acting between the state and the tiller of the soil. The promulgation of the Land Act in 1957 was intended to introduce some reforms, but it also generated fear among the land owners. Finally, as a result of the Land Act of 1957, a large number of cultivators and sharecroppers were evicted because the landowners were worried and attempted to safeguard their interests. Therefore, peasants were deprived of a means of production, due to the fear that the government intended to protect tenancy. The peasant organizations protested against such unfair practices,[54] but the interests of the landed aristocracy and lack of up to date land holding records further

53. Grishma Bahadur Devkota, *Nepalko Rajnaitik Darpan* (The Political Mirror of Nepal), Vol. III, Kathmandu : Umesh Bahadur Devkota, 2040 V.S. pp. 917-947.

54. *Report of The Land Reforms Commission,* Kathmandu : Land Reforms Commission, 1953, p. 2.

aggravated such problems. The *Birta* cultivators and tenants suffered greatly. The *Birta* owners usually did not issue *Bharpai* (receipt) upon payment of rent, which made it easy to evict tenants. The tenants also could not claim their tenancy rights due to a lack of written evidence.

After 1951, *Kut* was determined by the demand and supply of land. Only in 1955, did the government declare that all rent, taxes and levies would be collected according to existing statutes. The growing peasants' protests, especially in Bhaktapur district, reduced the rent. The most remarkable impact of such protests was that the *Birta* owners began to issue *Bharpai* (receipts issued by land owners upon payment of rent),[55] but in other parts of the country, rent was randomly fixed at the rate of one half of the gross produce. Thus, different rates prevailed in the country. Generally, the peasants retained only one third of the gross produce, but it was inadequate for subsistence. In this case, peasants were compelled to borrow loans from local moneylenders in order to pay rent to the *Birta* owners, *Jagirdars* or the *Guthi* institutions if the harvest was poor, but high rates of interest were charged on such loans. This forced many peasants to relinquish land to the moneylenders. Therefore, the Land Reforms Commission suggested for the owners to participate in the production process and to extend loans to cultivators in need at the rate of 10% interest.[56] The Land Reforms Act of 1964 brought about changes in the traditional land holding system and influenced the existing agrarian relations. Its goals were tenancy protection, the control of *Kut* rent and the abolition of levies. In this way it eradicated some of the feudal elements of the system, but various land problems remained without solutions. The situation required for those land tenure problems to be eradicated through the proper amendment of various land laws.

Changes in the Nature of Relationships :

The successful political movement against the Rana regime

55. Budhathoki, f.n. 8, pp. 41-43.
56. Devkota, f.n. 53-p. 943.

in 1951 immediately had several impacts on the agrarian system. The Nepalese peasantry pressurized the democratic government to introduce reforms in the existing agrarian systems, and consequently, various land laws were promulgated in the 1950s. Even before 1951, there were some of the *Sawals* (regulations) which dealt, to some extent, with the system.[57]

Even after the end of the Rana regime, several land related acts were also promulgated, and those laws attempted to reform the existing traditional systems. Domination of agrarian relations by the privileged classes and ruthless exploitation fueled discontent among the peasantry, which at once burst movements which pushed for changes in traditional types of agrarian structure and agrarian relations. Traditionalism and its impact on the society finally led to the promulgation of various land laws. The land laws promulgated from 1951 to 1964 brought about certain changes in existing agrarian relations.

In 1951, the Tenancy Rights Acquisition Act was drafted. The act as such had two consequences -

— The people who did not cultivate land were protected, but the actual cultivators, including sharecroppers, were denied such rights because they had no documentary evidence of cultivation, and

— It increased volume of tenancy rights transactions.

The major provisions of the proposed act were-

— Tenancy rights was given to those who cultivated land around 1951, without any consideration of the mode of land acquisition, such as- *Ukhada, Hunda, Kutbali, Khadebataiya, Mankhab, Nagadi,* etc.

— The landowners were prohibited from evicting tenants on *Ukhada, Hunda, Kutbali, Khadebataiya, Mankhab, Nagadi*, etc. unless they paid rent and taxes regularly.

— The landowners and tenants were required to fill out form

57. Those *Sawals* include *Pahad Malko Sawal, Madesh Malko Sawal, Jimidar Patuwarika Namko Sawal, Jimmawali Sawal, Muluki Sawal* and *Jimmawal Patuwaliko Sawal.*

called the *Ekchhape Kabuliyat* (single stamped bond), which was aimed at preventing them from mistreating the cultivators.

— The transfer of tenancy rights through sale and mortgage was restricted.

— The tenants were required to get permission from the owners prior to digging pits, wells, or building houses on such land.

Although implementation of the act was required, the landowning elite did not favour it and they united against the act. Consequently, the act was repealed.

The traditional type of *Ain Sawal* which was promulgated by the Rana rulers attempted to regulate agriculture and land administration without any hindrances before 1951, but was ineffective. In fact, the rulers did really intend to make any changes. Therefore, there was no substantial attempt to correct the society's defective structural patterns. The *Birta* owners and *Jagirdars* of vast areas of land tracts were either Ranas or their close friends. The major problems involved in land holding at the end of the Rana rule were insecurity of tenancy, rural indebtedness, the dishonesty of moneylenders and absenteeism.

This situation continued with no changes for almost a decade after end of the Rana rule. The promulgation of land laws during 1950s were very significant due to the introduction of changes in traditional relations. After 1964, the agrarian structure was modified; the eradication of several hierarchies of absentees and the end of intermediary practices introduced changes in production relations and raised the status of peasants by granting tenurial rights. All the laws promulgated until 1964 brought further changes in the agrarian structure and land tenure system. The diagram shows the production relations that prevailed at the end of the Rana's rule in Nepal (appendix-4).

The abolition of different traditional land tenures brought changes to the basic nature of the existing traditional type of relationship. Many absentees and intermediaries were abolished, which proved to be a relief for cultivating peasants and introduced remarkable changes to both agrarian relations and the agrarian social structure. It marked the beginning of social welfare of peasantry gradually, they were given incentives and their land rights were recognized after 1964. The changes that occurred in agrarian relation in late 1950s aimed at uplifting the peasantry and eventually guaranteeing their rights. The growing demand for change by peasants during the 1950s compelled the rulers to review their problems, the act of 1964 introduced basic changes in agrarian relations. The act guaranteed tenancy and occupancy rights, protection against arbitrary eviction, and regularized rent payments. All kinds of traditional levies were abolished by promulgating an act in 1951. Finally, the Land Reform Act brought owners and tenants and state and cultivators into a face to face relationship,[58] and further moderated agrarian relations. So, the act itself has been an epoch in bringing about changes in the traditional agriculture. However, the act did not bring total changes in traditional system. The beginning of changes in traditional agrarian relations and other aspects of agriculture has been significant in the study of agrarian system, but the role of the landowners has remained in tact until now. Even now they can obtain land ownership rights without performing any kind of duties to improve agriculture. Their rent collection rights are protected as before, but the rate of *Kut* previously exacted at the rate of one half of the total yield was reduced to one *muri* three *pathi* of rice on *Abal* land, which constituted almost 17% of the total yield. Also, *Kut* is payable only in the major crop, they could not exact rent in wheat crops, i.e. the winter crop. At the same time, the owners were required to issue receipts in the name of the tenants upon payment of rent. Refusal to do this was regarded as a breach of the law. The worst forms of tenurial practice, sharecropping and *Bataiya*, still remain in practice. Generally, in the sharecropping system, the total yield is divided into two haives between owners and cultivators. The land

58. *Bhumi Sambandhi Ain Ra Niyamharu* (Land Act and Regulations), Birat Nagar : Sahitya Prakashan, 2023 V.S., pp. 14-16.

owners and even the rich tenants rent land for cultivation to the sharecroppers because it is more profitable than cultivating by themselves. So, the community of sharecroppers continues to exist in the structural hierarchy. These sharecroppers had no written evidence with which to claim their rights. but if the owner issued receipts upon payment of rent or officially agreed with a cultivator, it became possible to obtain tenancy rights. But the overall situation now is changing to a greater degree than the system before 1951. Lastly, the Land Reforms Amendment Act of 1995 was intended to make complete changes in the agrarian relations, but it was affected by contemporary Nepalese politics. Even so, tenants are given ownership rights. In fact, this act brought about total changes in the nature of agrarian relations and structure as well. The tenancy was abolished and the ownership rights vested in the land owners was made divisible into two equal halves between owners and cultivators. In this way, occupancy rights are now converted into ownership rights.[59] All the tenants with occupancy right registered in the "field book" of the survey department are raised to the status of owners, which will certainly end tenancy. Nonetheless, still it does not eradicate the sharecropping system. Previously, all those tenants were represented by the owners, who dealt with the state, and this situation remains unchanged. But one thing is very clear that until now, nothing has been able to end illegal sharecropping practices. Although their status has been changed to that of owners, the sharecropping system still has far reaching consequences for the peasant subsistence economy and the fragmentation of holdings. Certain changes occurred in the structure of the society, which are shown in the chart (appendix. 5).

This chart makes clear that the cultivators community are no longer existed. All tenants now have the status of landowners, that is, owners of one half of area in which they hold tenancy rights. Legally, there are no tenants any more, although the

59. Land Act amendment 1995.

practice of sharecropping still exists. The rich landowners rent land to sharecroppers, who are required to pay one half of the total yield as contractual rent. The new land law was also unable to reform such kinds of medieval agricultural practice. In fact, the growing population and high pressure on the land, lack of other means of production, decline of the national economy, higher ratio of rural indebtedness etc. further contributed to the continuation of such practices in Nepalese agriculture even until recent times.

* * *

CHAPTER VI

CONCLUSION

A Newari folk song dated 869 N.S. (Nepal Sambat = 1749 A.D.) mentions that a land lord was attracted by the beauty of his tenant's wife. He wanted to seduce her, but she refused. He compelled her to surrender by threatening to change tenant.[1] Thus, there was no security in terms of land holding because landlords could evict tenants. This situation gives a clear picture of the agrarian situation in Nepal at that time, which did not witness significant changes until 1951.

Nepal has adapted varied agrarian systems since ancient times. Agrarian relations were determined by several factors, such as land holding, rent payment, taxes, and credit supply, but the land holding and revenue administration, land settlement, and the production process all changed little through the centuries. Nepalese society and its economy remained almost stagnant for centuries without any significant changes. Before the second half of the nineteenth Century, farmers and labourers were seldom distinctly separated, so only one term *Mohi* (tenant) was used to express their common conditions.

The English doctrine of rent at the rate of one-third or one-fourth of the gross product remained a legend both in India and Nepal. The rates of rent that were regulated in Nepal were determined by the indigenous traditional system. The revenue contractors made their contracts in direct consultation with the

1. T.R. Vaidya, *Prithvi Narayan Shah : The Founder of Modern Nepal*, New Delhi : Anmol Publication, 1993, p. 324.

government, so the *Thekedars* had to visit Kathmandu regularly. Before the contract expired, they summoned professional land measurers - the *Dongol*, *Khathet* and the *Patuwari* to measure the actual area under cultivation. The *Thekedaree* tax was fixed accordingly. The government exacted their share at the rate of 2 Anas to 4 Anas per rupee of collection. At that time, the contractors also played an important role in the country's rural activities. In addition to their regular duties, they acted as moneylenders. The practice of money lending is of great importance in the study of agrarian relations in Nepal. The landlords, intermediaries or local functionaries lent money to needy peasants especially for the purposes of weeding, the *shraddha*, or for observing festivals, rites and rituals. This situation continued even after 1846. Debts were contracted by the village farmers at the *Sawaee* rate, or 25% added interest. Similarly, in kind loans were also extended, for which the Sawaee interest rate was charged. Same rate was charged on loans in terms of seeds, cattle and plough. At that time, Sawaee interest rate was not considered to be excessive, but same rates were charged on debts even one hundred years later. The justification for the existence of *Sawaee* was the lack of collateral against which to contract loans for the needy peasants.

The process of monetization was very slow in nineteenth century Nepal, and the rural part of the country suffered greatly from it. Therefore, the lack of monetization and limited sources of credit supply created favourable conditions for the privileged classes. Consequently, the moneylenders charged higher rates of interest on every kind of debt that they extended. The act of money lending provided them with an opportunity to earn additional income and some other relative benefits. For poor farmers, it provided easy access to loans with which to perform family rituals or, to some extent, initiate production activities. The peasants paid interest at exorbitant rates, as desired by the moneylenders, and a debtor was also required to offer gifts in kind like vegetables, fruit, milk, fuel wood, etc. Sometimes, the money-lenders also ordered debtors to do specific household work for them.

The agrarian system in Nepal has specific features. The system that existed during the Rana rule was linked to the system that had been adapted by their predecessors in one way or another, but the agrarian history and agrarian relations under them showed some changes in comparison to the system that prevailed before 1846. But the basic features of the agricultural system remained intact. The landlords, absentees, intermediaries, Ijaredars (revenue contractors), and local revenue functionaries all contributed to the dominance of, and dependency upon the peasant community while exploiting agricultural resources. The privileged class, in general, did not cultivate land by themselves. They instead rented it to prospective cultivators and exacted agricultural surpluses in the form of rent, taxes and levies. Furthermore, they were also permitted to exact Beth-begar in the form of free labour services from each peasant household. On the contrary, they had no role or participation in the entire production process. They neither provided seeds, fertilizer, nor financial support in order to increase production and improve the land. They contacted the tenant-cultivators only at the time of rent collection. The peasants used family labour or cultivated land through the *Parma* (exchange of labour). They performed all of the required work and incurred expenses for the entire production process. At that time, the system was such that they had to pay higher rates of rent, taxes and levies. This situation was equally applied on all *Raikar, Guthi, Jagir* and *Birta* lands, but the peasants in the Kathmandu valley found the payment of *Guthi* rent to be the cruelest system, although all the rates were more or less similar. In fact, the rulers did not pay attention to the peasants' condition particularly because of political reasons. The landlords were the main supporters of the rulers, thus, by virtue of customs and statutes, the landowners claimed and exacted their share in the agrarian produce at exorbitant rates. The high rates of rent, free labour services, and the existing socio-economic and agricultural systems all made the peasant community vulnerable and compelled them to live under bare subsistence conditions.

The rights of peasant-cultivators were not well defined due to the lack of records concerning cultivators' rights. During the Rana regime, there had been fixed rates or sharecropping tenancies. The *Kut* system, or the fixed rate tenancy, was not favourable for the peasants, because they had to pay a fixed amount for rent under all conditions, including crop failure. Therefore, the sharecropping tenancy was favourable for them because gross produce was divided into two halves regardless of production. The century long Rana regime could not improve peasants' conditions. It was only in 1957 that some relief was granted after rent was fixed at the standard level, but the *Kut* rates and government revenue largely differed. The *Raikar* landowners exacted 1 *Muri* 3 *pathi* of rice as *Kut*, whereas they paid just a nominal amount to the government. However, in kind collection constituted approximately Rs. 725.00. This situation existed even after the promulgation of the Land Reforms Act in 1964, and this disparity required proper reforms. From 1846 to 1951, various *Sanads, Sawals, Rukkas* etc were issued which dealt with different aspects of the land holding system but these measures also failed to improve cultivators' conditions. There was no uniform decision on land problems as the orders of the Rana Premiers varied according to their whim in each case. This situation remained intact due to the lack of proper land legislation, geophysical conditions, and political reasons. It was obvious that a large number of absentees who belonged to the aristocracy and nobility were favoured by the rulers, which finally led to inconsistencies in the agricultural system. Thus, sometimes, the orders of the Premiers were neither impartial nor effective, and the peasant cultivators were oppressed mercilessly by the renting class. The traditional agrarian system did not witness significant changes right after the end of the regime, so it is not an exaggeration to say that peasants in Nepal were born in fields, produced grain for squire and gentry and died in the fields. There were no protest movements by the peasant community against the land owning elite during the Rana regime, but after reform measures were initiated in 1951, a series of peasant movements were organized to fight against traditional practices. Similarly, peasant organizations were established. They protested against the unjust agricultural system and its injustices. The ineffectiveness of the Land Act of 1957 allowed the traditional system to remain in operation in most parts of the country, but the Birta Abolition Act and Land Reforms Act were the landmarks in the agrarian history of Nepal. Consequently, protection was granted against arbitrary eviction. It was made possible only through a Court of Law. It also fixed the level of rent, taxes and levies, and confirmed the rights of the involved parties. The Land Reforms Act was to be implemented on a phase wise basis in the districts. Most of the old hierarchies were eradicated from the rungs of the agrarian structure, but the basic form of land and agrarian structure and agrarian relations remained almost the same. In Nepal, the cultivating tenants were not given significant land rights during or after the Rana regime. Before 1951, it was very common for the cultivators to be able to retain cultivation rights as long as they paid rent and taxes regularly, but if they failed to pay it for three consecutive years, a cultivator could be evicted through a court of law. The act of 1964 limited the time allowed for eviction, but regardless of the rules, the tenant cultivators were evicted as frequently as possible by the land owners. The bidding system prevalent in the *Birta* holdings also strengthened the system very much and helped to ruin the peasant economy. The existing system registered two people in a particular piece of *Raikar* land as the tax paying land owner (registered as tenants) and the cultivating tenant as the sharecroppers. The registered tenants were given all possible land rights. They held land ownership and property rights, whereas the later cultivated land and paid rent. According to the Act of 1964, the eviction process was to be started either through the Village *Panchayat* or the court of law depending on the nature of charges made against the cultivators. The peasants' rights were highly limited. The transfer of tenancy rights through sale was prohibited by the promulgation of the Land Reforms

Act in 1964. Now, it is limited and could be transferred to whichever son of the *Mohi* that the landowner trusts.[2] The internal practice of property division made it possible to divide land among the sons, but it was to be registered in the name of only one of the cultivator's trusted sons. However, it was necessarily transferred to the owners if a tenant died without any legitimate heirs. Contemporary land holding practices have created various controversial issues. This situation requires proper reforms in the agrarian system in order to bring about changes in the basic nature of agrarian relations.

As mentioned above, various land systems have been in existence in Nepal for many centuries and some have a long historical tradition. The major forms of tenure include the *Raikar, Birta, Guthi, Jagir, Rakam* and *Kipat. Basically, Raikar* and *Kipat* were the two main forms of land tenure. The *Raikar* is considered to be government land, whereas *Kipat* was communal land (of the Limbus and other minor ethnic groups). The other forms of tenure were created from *Raikar* itself through the transfer of rights by the state or individual owners. The state granted its land rights to individuals or institutions on different occasions, and it created individuals' land rights. The tax exempt grants deprived the state of land taxes, and all incomes were accrued by the individual grantees, but this type of tenure was abolished after the end of the Rana's rule.

Land holding practices varied in different tenures. The state as the owner of *Raikar* land, is the biggest landlord. The registered tenants were considered to be the land owners on *Raikar* land and paid taxes to the government. Sometimes, they cultivated land by themselves whereas in some *Raikar*, it was cultivated by the *Mohi* (the cultivating tenants) who paid rent in kind to the owner. The owners accrued a large part of profit from the rent and paid only an insignificant amount to the state as land revenue. The state's rights were waived in favour of

2. *Bhumi Sambandhi Ain Tatha Niyamharu 2021 V.S.*, (Land Act and Regulations 2021), Birtnagar : Nepali Sahitya Bhandar, 2023 V.S. pp. 12-16.

individuals on *Jagir* and *Birta* land, so most of the *Birta* land, which was granted to individuals was tax exempt for life time or for ever. The *Birta* cultivators paid higher rates of rent to the *Birta* owners in the form of rice, semi-milled rice, and various special levies. In general, the condition of peasants was unsatisfactory as they were exploited by the land owning elite to the extent that they were compelled to live under bare subsistence conditions.

Guthi land was granted to religious or philanthropic institutions by individuals or by the state, and was managed by the *Guthiyars* (trustee members). The particular institution collected rent in kind and cash and spent it for the purposes that the donor intended it for at the time of grant. Such activities generally included worship, water supplies for visitors, public shelter management, managing orphanages, feasting, donating for charitable purposes, celebrating festivals, regulating worship maintaining the temples etc. Generally, *Guthi* land was tax exempt, but on rare occasions some kinds of *Guthi* land were also taxable.

Land holding practices also varied for the *Raikar* and *Kipat* tenures. The *Kipat* was communal land which had been granted to the *Limbus* in eastern Nepal and to some other ethnic groups in other parts of the country.

The rent composition, cultivation conditions, landowners' rights, absentees, intermediaries and cultivators, status and position of village moneylenders in rural societies, interest rates, land mortgage, and household peasant economy were directly related to the nature of agrarian relations in Nepal under the Ranas. Of course, the peasant cultivators played a vital role in agricultural production activities. However, they were placed at the lowest rung of the agrarian hierarchy. They were denied adequate land rights during the Rana regime, and their role in production activities was appreciated neither by the state nor by the land owners. Extreme poverty forced peasants to work in the fields even under the most unfavourable conditions. Their relationship with the land owning elite was mainly determined by financial terms rather than by socio-cultural factors, and agricultural traditions strongly influenced the relations between various groups. The conditions of the peasantry are closely related to the nature of agrarian relations to some extent; rent and taxes remained vital in the relationship, and the tenants paid one half of the gross produce as rent. In fact, the peasant cultivators paid one to one *Muri* 10 *Pathi* of semi-milled rice and 5 *Pathis* to 30 *Pathis* of wheat per *Ropani* of land regardless of production. In addition to this, they were required to pay *Salami*, such as wheat and rice straw, red and white soil with which to paint houses, straw mats, barely, free porter services, and other jobs which were required by the owners. The *Guthi* rent was comparatively higher and tougher for the peasants. In some places, including some parts of the Kathmandu valley, the *Guthi* rent was higher than the rates prescribed for adjoining *Raikar* holdings. The *Guthi* rent was fixed at the rate of 37.4 *Pathis* of rice per *Ropani* of land. Around 1950, one Ropani of the best land in the Kathmandu valley produced only 2 to 4 *Muris* (1 *muri* = 2 mounds) (40 to 80 *Pathi*) of rice. There was less fertile land which could produce only 2.5 *Muri* of rice, and which was designated *Guthi*. The intermediaries were permitted to retain 2 *Pathis* 4 *Manas* to 17 *Pathis* 4 *Manas* of rice as their share. But in *Birta*, the peasants sometimes requested for the *Birta* owners to reduce rent and consequently, a kind hearted *Birta* owner from the ruling elite might sometimes make a small reduction. In the *Guthi* tenure, however, inhumane means were sometimes used to collect rent, and no concessions were granted, so this system became a burden for the cultivators. In response to unjust practices, the Tirobandi Andolan (the movement for non-payment of rent) was organized in order to eradicate the *Guthi* and mobilize the peasants against rent payment. This movement compelled the government to declare a 13 point reform plan. The 'Andolan' itself was a major step against excessive payments, during which the peasant activists complained and prevented other peasants from carrying sacks of rice to deliver as rent to the *Guthi* institution or the *Birta* owners.[3] In 1953, the *Kut* of the *Guthi* was reduced to 1 *Muri* 5 *Pathis* of which one-third was payable in cash at the rate of Rs. 6.0 per *Muri*. This step was also considered to be of aid to the peasant community, but the customary levies and *Rakams* (labour and other material obligatio) were payable at the old rates. The Sauneyfagu rates were Rs. 0.07 to 0.14 respectively.[4] The high level of discontent before 1951 as well as the desire to bring about a prosperous future finally led to the establishment of various peasant organizations in Nepal, such as the *Krishi Sudhar Sangh* (KKS), *Akhil Nepal Kisan Sangh* (ANKS), *Akhil Nepal Suddhikarn Kisan Sangh* (ANSKS)), and *Bhumijiwi Sangh* (BJS). In fact, the land owners were very powerful, and the state favoured them for political reasons. They could detain peasants if they defaulted on payments. This situation compelled peasant organizations to put forward the following demands—

— Land ownership belongs to the government. Therefore, land taxes should be paid only to the government and not to the individual owners, and

— Land should belong to those who cultivate it. Land rights should be given to those who plough the land.

For centuries, there was no farmers' movement to boost production. Similarly, no peasant movements were organized before 1951. However, peasants movements were basically confined to rent, peasant 'welfare, land distribution, and the abolition of levies. The leftist movements devoted themselves to the peasant welfare and claimed to safeguard their interests,

---

3. Padma Bahadur Budhathaki, *Nepalma Kisan Andolan* (Peasant Movements in Nepal), Bhaktapur : The Author, 2048, V.S., pp. 86-90.
4. Krishna Bhakta Chauguthi, *Kisanko Avastha* (Conditions of Peasants), Bhaktapur : The Author, 2043 V.S., pp. 5-15.
5. *Suddhikaran Kisan Sanghko Ghosana Patra* (Penifesto of All Nepal Peasants' Purification Association), Somlingtar : Publicity Department-Central Office, 2007.

so, the leaders also demanded the abolition of the feudal and semi-feudal elements that were still prevalent. The Land Reforms Commission also agreed upon and approved six popular demands of the *Suddhikaran Kisan Sangh,*[6] which was originally put forward by the Krishi Sudhar Sangh (Agricultural Reforms Association) led by Padma Bahadur Budhathoki. Those demands include-

— Land must be given to them who cultivate it.

— To replace in kind rent assessment by the cash assessment.

— All *Rakams* payable to the land owners must be canceled.

— Distribute land to the cultivators.

— Provide foods to the poor cultivators, and

— Give land to the landless for subsistence.

The suppression of the peasants and traditional agricultural exploitation continued nonetheless. In 1952, The *Krishi Sudhart Sangha* and the *Akhil Nepal Kisan Sangh* jointly agreed to put forward following demands-

— Abolish all kins of exploitations of the peasant community.

— The land owners' share in the gross produce must be fixed on the basis of existing rules.

— The Rakams and the Salami levied on Birta land must be abolished, and

— Provide irrigation facilities to increase production.[7]

Then the government planned to supres the peasant movements and sent a police force to Somlingtar, where the central office of the *Suddhikarn Kisan Sangh* was based. This created terror among the peasants in the rural areas in the

6. For details on demands See : *Pamphlet of the ANSKS* 2011 V.S., Also See : Budhathoki, f.n. 3., pp. 30-34.
Shanker Thapa, "Peasant discontent, Consciousness and the Demand for Change," *Voice of History,* Vol. XIV, No. 1, June 1999, p. 48.
7. Thapa, f.n. 6, pp. 48-49.

Kathmandu valley. The majority of the peasants in rural Kathamndu supported the peasant leadership of Padma Bahadur Budhathoki and joined forces with him. The government could not resist the pressure of the ANSKS. This brought about immediate changes which benefited the peasants; for example, the then government agreed to extend the time limit for rent payments. The rent payable in rice was reduced, in kind rent was made payable at government rates, and Guthi rent was also made payable half in cash and half in kind. It was also permitted to deposit rent at the *Mal Adda* if the land owners refused to accept rent from the cultivators irrespective of the reason. Similarly, amount of rent in adjoining *Raikar* and *Guthi* tenures in the Kathmandu valley was declared uniform. Before this decision was made the rent varied from place to place, and was not properly regulated. These were the changes that the activities of peasant leader Padma Bahadur Budhathoki compelled the government to introduce. The peasant leaders made the tenants more active and gave impetus to their leadership by putting forward more demands. They organized several demonstrations and their leaders were arrested in an attempt to suppress the movement.[8] The professional peasants' organizations intended to bring about changes in agriculture and expected to improve the cultivators' condition, so, various movements were organized against unfair or illegal practices. The Nepali Congress also worked to improve the conditions of the peasant community.[9]

The changes in rent policies granted relief to the peasant cultivators, as the new amounts charged were much more moderate than the previous ones. In 1964, a survey was conducted in different districts, which measured land areas and determined the rent accordingly. The old system of rent assessment was canceled when the new act went into effect.

8. Ram Bahadur Jyapu, *Nepalma Kisan Andolan* (Peasant Movement in Nepal), Kathmandu : Yuva Sahitya Prakashan, n.d., pp. 1-50.
9. *Nepali Congressley Kisnharuko Lagi Ke Garyo ?* (What has the Nepali Congress Done for the Pesants ?): Kathmandu : The Nepali Congress, n.d., pp. 12-14.

But it too, could not satisfy the peasant community, which began to demand that tenancy rights should be made salable, transferable, and divisible among the heirs of the *Mohi* in order to guarantee more benefits.[10] During the Rana regime, the lack of proper land measurement legislation allowed owners to manipulate the actual land area that had been cultivated, so, the cultivators paid *Kut* for considerably larger areas than they actually cultivated. The Communists organized meaningful peasant movements, particularly in the *Tarai* districts, against unjust landlords and moneylenders, but in most cases, the movements resulted in violent clashes.[11] The large number of people involved in such clashes and movements raised the issues of rates of rent, tenancy rights, the eviction of tenants, opposition to the compulsory saving scheme, starvation, maltreatment by the landlords, exploitation and so on. The conflicts occurred between landlords and tenants, police and villagers, landlords and villagers and the government and peasants. The three-fourth of such cases occurred in the Tarai, which was due to the fact that it had the highest concentration of tenants in the region. The peasant uprising in Jhapa district was the most violent way in which the peasants expressed their feelings against the landowning elite, but the leaders of the movement were arrested and the government suppressed the movement, which was organized by one of the most influential communist factions in Nepal. In certain other conflicts, police force was deployed to suppress the protesters. Consequently, many peasants were killed. The nature of the land owning elite's activities against the peasant protesters shows that there was an inter-class alliance between the landlords and the rulers. The rival forces were always the poor peasants, the village women, and the

10. *Ibid.*, p. 30.
11. Jyapu, f.n. 8, pp. 1-50.
Also see : Sushil Raj Pandey, *The Political Economy of Land Reforms—Some Aspects,* Kathmandu : Himalayan Pioneers for Public Service and Research, 1985, pp. 145-148.

tenants.[12] In some districts, even 39 years after the promulgation of the Land Reforms Act has still not been implemented, and the old traditions and statutes continue to function.[13] One person is registered as a tax payer and the cultivating tenant shares rights with the other party, but the cultivating peasants' rights are very limited. They could claim property rights only on the one fourth of the total land area that they cultivated, and at the same time, the distribution of land was also unequal. However, this practice of the divison of property right has been modified. Consequently, the tenant cultivators got property right on one half of the total area.

The Rana regime failed to promulgate land laws. The *Rukkas, Sanads* and *Sawals*, which dealt with land related matters were inadequate for regulating land relations, but after 1951, various land laws were promulgated which dealt with different aspects of Nepalese agriculture.

All the laws had some impact on the agrarian system in the country. The old system needed to be reformed in order to correspond to modern realities. The Land Reforms Commission analyzed the agricultural conditions and proposed reforms in 1962, but it did not favour the popular demand of *land* to *the tiller* proposed by the peasant activists.[14] The land records clearly distinguished between registered tenants and cultivators. Such a distinction has contributed to exploitation by intermediaries and the registered tenants or the land owners were categorized as such acting between the state and the tillers of the soil. The promulgation of the Land Act of 1957 was intended to make some reforms, but created fear among the

---

12. *Ibid.*, pp. 158-161.
    Also See : Fredrick H. Gaige, *Regionalism and National Unity in Nepal,* New Delhi : Vikas publishing House, 1975, pp. 172-177.
13. *A Draft Proposal On Programmes of Agricultural Revolution In Nepal Coounist Party UML 2049 V.S.,* Katmandu : NCP UML Central Office, 2049 V.S. pp. 3-5.
14. Grishma Bahadur Devkota, *Nepalko Rajnaitik Darpan* (The Political Morror of Nepal) Vol, III, Kathmandu : Umesh Bahadur Devkota, 2040, pp. 917-947.

land owners, that the government intended to protect tenancy. Consequently a large number of cultivators and sharecroppers were evicted and deprived of a means of production. But the peasant organizations protest did not fail to protest against such unjust eviction.[15] Of course, the interests of the landed aristocracy and lack of up to date land holding records worsened such problems. The *Birta* cultivators suffered more than any others, the *Birta* owners usually did not issue *Bharpai* (receipts) on payment of rent, which meant that there was no written evidence of cultivation, and this made it easy for them to evict tenants. The tenants also could not claim tenancy rights due to the lack of such evidence.

After 1951, *Kut* was occasionally determined by the economic principle of demand and supply of land. Only in 1955 did the government decide to collect rent, taxes and levies in correspondence with existing statutes. The growing peasant protests, especially in *Bhaktapur* district, compelled the government to reduce rent. Formerly, the *Birta* cultivators used to pay 4 to 6 *Muri* of rice or 2 to 3 *Muri* of milled rice per *Ropani*. Sometimes, they could not produce that much rice and defaulted on payments. But the most remarkable impact of such protests was that the *Birta* owners began to issue *Bharpai* upon payment of rent, which provided evidence with which to claim tenancy rights.[16] But in other parts of the country, rent was fixed at the rate of one half of the gross produce. This proves that different rates of rent prevailed in the country. Under ordinary conditions, the *Raikar* peasants could retain only one third of the gross produce, but it was inadequate for subsistence. Furthermore, the peasants in the Kathmandu valley were compelled to take loans from local moneylenders in order to

---

15. *Ibid.*, p. 920. Also see : Bhumi Sambandhi Ain 2014 V.S. (Land Act 1957), *Nepal Kanon Patrika,* Vol. VI, No. 8, Kathmandu, The Supreme Court, pp. 192-198., Also see : *Nepal Gazette,* Pt. VII, No. 5 (Extraordinary), 22 Shrawan, 2014.
Report of The Land Reforms Commission, Kathmandu: Department of Land Reforms, 1953, pp. 18-27.
16. Budhathoki, f.n. 3, pp. 41-43 and 114-115.

pay rent to the landowners in the event of a bad harvest, as well as contracting loans for household expenses. Exorbitant rates of interest were charged on such loans, Which finally compelled the debtors to transfer occupancy rights. Therefore the Land Reforms Commission also suggested for landowners to participate in the production process, and attempted to end the 'honeymoon' involving the separation of cultivation and land ownership. In fact, the unity of land ownership and cultivation has always proved to be very significant for the agrarian production relations, and separation of these two is in no way positive for agrarian production relations and production itself. The lack of cultivators' rights ultimately leads to the deterioration of production activities. The commission further suggested that they should extend loans to cultivators in need at 10 percent interest.[17] The Land Reforms Act of 1964 brought about changes in the traditional land holding system, which also influenced the existing pattern of agrarian relations. The Act was intended to provide tenancy protection, control *Kut* rent, create land rights, and abolish various types of customary levies. In other words, its purpose was to eradicate some of the feudal aspects of land ownership, but various land problems remained the same even decades after its promulgation. The situation made it necessary to eradicate such defects in land tenure through the proper amendment of various land laws and promulgation of new ones.

The institutionalization of peasant society was strengthened after 1951, and their concerted activities, and political motivation placed strong pressure on the regime. The prevailing traditional agricultural practices, along with inability of the act of 1964 to grant adequate rights to peasant-cultivators, further compelled the government to pay more attention to improving the conditions of the peasantry. During the totalitarian *Panchayat* regime (1960-1990), the peasant activists combined political ideology with the peasants' interests and welfare. The peasants consciousness and overwhelming impact of

17. Devkota, f.n. 14,p. 943.

communist ideology furthered the demand for basic changes in both the agrarian social structure and agrarian relations. This is the reason why the demand of *"land to the tiller"* has become more popular. The leaders motivated them to believe that they were the ones who could bring a golden age of justice and equality, and always coined inspirational slogans while promoting the idea of *"land to the tiller"*.

In fact, the protection of landlords by the regime and vulnerable conditions of the peasantry led to rising dissatisfaction among them. They could not strive for a better future during the Rana regime, but the end of the regime brought about significant changes in the peasants' activities. Starting first after 1951, and then continuing until 1960. This was the result of the old agriculture system, but it has had far reaching consequences for Nepal's agrarian society and economy.

* * *

BIBLIOGRAPHY

A. PRIMARY

Unpublished

Archival Records

— Guthi Corporation records
— Ministry of Law and Justice records
— Record Section (*Lagat Phant*) of the Department of Revenue, Dillibazar HMG/N.
— Records of the *Badahakim's* office of Birganj *Goswara* the Zonal Commissioner's office of Narayani *Zone*
— Papers of National Archives of Nepal, Kathmandu.
— Records of *Gwoswara-Tahabil*, Kathmandu.
— Bhaktapur *Mal Adda* Records, Kathmandu.
— *Jaishi Kotha* Records in *Charkhal Adda*/Dillibazar, Kathmandu.

Published

Rules, Regulations Laws Etc.

— Agricultural Rent Act 1955.
— The *Ain* - 1992 B.S.(1935).
— Administrative Regulations for Jumla-1900.
— Bhaktapur *Talukdari* Regulations.
— *Bhumi Sambandhi Ain Ra Niyamharu* (Land Act and Regulations), BiratnNagar: Sahitya Prakashan, 2023 B.S.
— *Birta Unmulan Ain* (Birta Abolition Act) 1959 and Amendments of 1960, 1962 and 1993.

— Birtawarley Birtama Rakam Lagai Linakhana Napauney Ain (Prohibition on Imposition of Rakam in Birta Land by the Birta Owners) 2015 B.S..
— Relevant Volumes of Nepal Gazettes.
— *Guthi* Corporation Act - 1972.
— *Jimidar Patuwari Ko Sawal* (Regulations for the Jimidar -Patuwari)..
— *Jimmawali Sawal*. (Regulations for Jimmawals).
— Land Act - 1957
— Land Regulations 1960
— Land Acquisition Act 1961
— Land Reforms Act 1964
— *Madhesh Jilla Jilla Ka Jimidar Patuwari Ka Nam Ko Sawal*, (Regulations for Jimidar- Patuwari in Tarai Districts), Kathmandu: Gorkhapatra,Press,2012 B.S.
— *Madhesh Mal Ko Sawal* (Tarai Revenue Regulations), Kathmandu, Ministry of Justice, 1954 .
— *Muluki Ain* (Civil Code)1910 B.S.(1854 A.D.) and its subsequent amendments, *Muliki Ain* 1988 B.S. (1931 A.D.) , 1992 B.S.(1935 A.D.).
— *Muluki Ain* (Civil Code) 2012, 2020 (1955 and 1963.
— *Nepal Ain Sangraha* (Collection of Nepal Acts) 7A, Kathmandu: Kanoon Kitab Byabastha Samiti, 2043 (1986 A.D.).
— *Pahad Mal Ko Sawal* (Revenue Regulations for the Hills) 1961.
— Rent and Tenancy Legislation in Birta - 1906 .
— The Royal Declaration of 1960 .

Manuscript, Research Reports ,Unpublished Dissertations And Party Publications :

In English

— *A Study of Bonded Labour,* Kathmandu: Ministry of Labour and Welfare, n.d., (Mimeorgraphed report)
— Banstola, Kedar Nath, 'Land Revenue Administration In Nepal', Ph.D. Dissertation University of Poona, 1985.

— *Draft Proposal on Agricultural Revolution in Nepal,* Kathmandu: NCPUML, 2049 B.S. (1992 A.D.).

— *Land Tenure Conditions In Eastern Nepal*, Kathmandu: Land Reforms Commission, 1953.

— *Land Tenure Connditions In Western Tarai*, Kathmandu: Land Reforms Commission, 1953.

— *Report On The Land Tenure Conditions in Western Nepal*, Kathmandu: Land Reforms Commission, 1953.

— *Report On Land Tenure Conditions in Saptari, Mahottari* and *Sarlahi,* Kathmandu: Land Reforms Commission, 1953.

— *Report On The Land Reforms Commission*, Kathmandu: 1953.

— *Report On The Land Reforms Commission of Bengal, Calcutta*: Government of Bengal, 1940

— *Royal Commission on Agriculture Report*, Bombay: Government Central Press, 1928.

— Scholtz, J.T., 'Policy Process and Rural Development: A Study of Land Reforms In Nepal', Berkeley: University of California, 1977. (Un Published Ph.D. dissertation).

— *Second Report of The Land Reforms Commission*, Kathmandu: Land Reforms Commission, 1953.

— Sharma, G.D, 'Zamindars and Land Rights in South Gujarat During the 18th Century', Unpublished Seminar Paper, Poona, Department of History, n.d.

— Shivanna, K.S., 'The Agrarian Relations With Special Reference To Revenue Terms As Reflected in Kannada Inscriptions During The 17the and 18th Centuries', Poona, Department of History- University of Poona, (Unpublished Seminar Paper).

— Uprety, Bed Prakash, 'Limbu-Brahman Interrelationship In Limbuwan Nepal', University of Wisconsin at Madison, 1975, (Unpublished Ph.D. Dissertation).

In Nepali

— Acharya, Babu Ram, Nepal Ma Jamin Ko Byavastha, (Unpublished manuscript)

— *Akhil Nepal Kisan Sangh Ko Ghosana Patra Ra Nitiharu,* Kathmandu: ANKS, 2047 (1992 A.D.).

— *Suddhikaran Kisan Sangh Ko Ghosana Patra* - 2007 (1951 A.D.)

— *Nepali Congressle Kisanharuko Lagi Ke Garyo*?, Kathmandu, Nepali Congress, n.d.

— *A.N.K.S. ko Karyakramharu* (Program of the ANKS) Kathmandu, ANKS Central Committee, n.d.

B. SECONDARY SOURCES:

Books, Journal Articles And Newspapers

Books in English

— Akhtar, Shirin, *The Roles of Zamindars In Bengal,* Dhaka: The Asiatic Society of Bangladesh, 1982.

— Andrus, J. Russel, *Burmese Economic Life*, Bombay: Oxford University Press, 1957.

— Baden-Powel, BH, *Indian Village Community,* Delhi: Cosmo Publication, 1972.

— Banstola, Kedar Nath, Taxation in Nepal : Special Reference to Revenue System, New Delhi: R.D. Publications, 1995.

— Beteille, Andre, Caste, Class and Power- Changing Pattern of Stratification In A Tanjore Village, Berkeley: University of California Press, 1965.

— -------------, *Studies In Agrarian Social Structure*, New Delhi: Oxford University Press, 1974.

— Birrel, Robert, Obstacle of Development In Peasant Societies - An Analysis of India, England and Japan', In Bock , Philip (ed.), *Peasants In The Modern World*, New Mexico: The University of New Mexico Press. 1969.

— Bock, Philip, Peasants In The Modern World, New Mexico: University of New Mexico Press. 1969.

— Brewer, Anthony, *Marxist Theories of Imperialism,* London: Roulette and Kegan Paul, 1989.

— Caplan, Lionel, *Land And Social Change In Eastern Nepal*, Berkeley: University of California Press, 1970.

— Chalise, Nava Raj, "Land Tenure and Tenancy In Nepal, in Report on National Seminar on Land Reforms in *Nepal*, Kathmandu: n.p. 1970

— Darling, M.L. *Punjab Peasants In Prosperity And Debt,* Oxford: The Oxford University Press.

— Fornier, Peter, *Land Reforms and Economic Development*, Middle Sex: Penguin books, 1972.

— Dutt, R.C, *The Economic History of India*, New Delhi: Ministry of Broadcasting and information, 1960.

— F.A.O., Land Reforms: *Land Settlements and Cooperatives*, Rome: UN Food And Agricultural Organization, 1981.

— F.A.O. -I.L.O., Progress In *Land Reforms,* New York: U.N.O., 1974.

— Fournier, Allain, "The Role of Priest In The Sunuwar Society", In Jim Fisher (ed.), *Himalayan Anthropology,* The Hague: Mouton, 1978.

— Fryekenberg, Robert Eric, *Land Tenure and Peasants In South Asia*, New Delhi: Manohar Publications, 1984.

— Galey, Jean-Claude, "Creditors, King and Debt", in Malmoud Charles (ed.), *Debts and Debtors*, New Delhi: Vikas Publishing House, 1983.

— Gunn, Geoffrey C., *Rebellion in Laos: Peasants in a colonial Bank Water,* Boulder: West View Press, 1990.

— Gupta, Sulekh Chandra, *Agrarian Relations And British Rule In India*, Bombay: Asia Publishing House, 1963.

— Gurung, Ganesh Man, *Chepang: A Study of Continuity and Change*, Kathmandu, S.B.Shah, 1988.

— Habib, Irfan, *The Agrarian System of Mughal India*, Bombay: Asia Publishing House, 1963.

— Hamilton, Francis Buchanon, *An Account of The District of Purnea*, Patna: Bihar and Orrisa Research Society, 1928.

— ------------, *An Account of The Kingdom of Nepal and of the Territories Anexed by the House of Gorkha,* New Delhi: Manju Sri Publishing House, 1971.

— Hassan, S. Nural, *Thoughts on Agrarian Relations in*

Mughal India, New Delhi: Motilal Benarsidass, 1993.

— Herring, Ronald J., 'Land Tenure and Credit Capital Tenure', in Robert E. Fryekenberg, *Land Tenure and Peasants In South Asia*, New Delhi: Manohar Publications. 1977.

— Iyengar, S. Keshavan, *Studies In Indian Rural Economics*, London: P.S. King and Sons, 1927.

— Jacobs, A.C. 'Landlords and Tenants', in R.A. Selligmann (ed.), *Encyclopaedia of The Social Science*, Vol. 9, New York: Mac Millan Co., 1957.

— Johnson Webster and Barlowe, Releigh, *Land Problem and Policies*, New York: Mac Million Co, 1954.

— Lakshminarayan, H. and Tyagi, S.S., *Changes In Agrarian Structure In India*, New Delhi: Agricole Publishing Academy, 1982.

— Landon, Perceval, Nepal 2 Vols, Kathmandu: Ratna Pustak Bhandar, 1976.

— Laski, Harold J., The Communist *Manifesto*: *The Socialist Landmark, London*: George Allen and Unwin, 1961

— Lenin, Vladimir I., "The Last Value", *Selected Works*, Vol. 18, Moscow: Progress Publisher, 1973.

— Littman, E.L., 'The Dynamics of Agriculture In Europe', in UN F.A.O., (ed.), *The Dynamics of Agriculture In Europe WACARD -The Year of Follow Up No. 10, 1978-88,* Rome: Food and Agricultural Organization, 1988.

— Majumdar, R.C. *etal, An Advanced History of India*, Mardas: Mcmillian India Ltd., 1985.

— Malmoud, Charies (ed.), *Debt and Debtors*, New Delhi: Vikas Pulbishing House, 1983.

— Malaviya, H.D., *Land Reforms In India*, New Delhi: All India Congress Committee, 1955.

— Marillat, H.C.R., *Land and The Constitution In India*, New York: Columbia University Press, 1970.

— Maotse Tung, "Report on an Investigation of Peasant Movements in Hunan", in *Selected Works of Maotse Tung*, Vol. I, Peking: Foreign Language Press, 1967.

— Meyer, Eric, "From Internal To External Debt" in Charles

Malmoud (ed.), *Debt and Debtors*; New Delhi: Vikas Publishing House, 1983.

— Mishra, G.P., *Some Aspects of Change In Agrarian Relations* (Institute of Socio-economic change Monograph no. 4), New Delhi: Sterling Publisher, 1977.

— Moore, Barington, *Origin of Dictatorship and Democracy: Lords And Peasants In the Making of The Modern World*, Middlesex: Penguin Books, 1966.

— Mooreland, W.H., *Agrarian System of Muslim India*, Allahabad: Central Book Depot, 1929.

— ---------, *India At The Death of Akbar*, Delhi: Atma Ram and Sons, 1962.

— Moore, Frank J, *Report on Land Tenure Conditions in Western Nepal*, Kathmandu: Ministry of Land Reforms, 1957.

— Mukharjee, Radha Kamal, "Land Tenure", in Edwin R.A. Selligmann, (ed.), *Encyclopaedia of The Sciences, IX-X*, New York: Mac Millan Co. 1957.

— Pal. N.M., *Some socio-eonomic Aspect of Land System of Bengal,* Calcutta: the Book company, 1929.

— Pandey, Sushil Raj, *The Political Economy of Nepalese Land Reforms*, Kathmandu: Himalayan Pioneers for Public Service and Research, 1985.

— Pouchapdass, Jacques, "Peasants' Debt in Colonial Bihar", in charles Malmoud (ed.), *Debt and Debtors*, New Delhi: Vikas Publishing House, 1983.

— Rahman, Atiur, *Peasant and Classes: A Study of Differentiation in Bangladesh, Delhi:* Vikas Publishing House, 1986.

— Rai, Navin K., *The People of Stone: The Chepangs of Central Nepal,* Kathmandu: Center for Nepal And Asian Studies, 1985.

— Rana, Padma Jung Bahadur, *Life of Maharaja Sir Jung Bahadur Rana*, Allahabad: The Pioneer Press, 1929.

— Regmi, Mahesh chandra, *Landownership In Nepal, Berkeley*: University of California Press, 1976.

— ----------, *Land Tenure and Taxation In Nepal, Kathmandu*: Ratna Pustak Bhandar, 1978.

— -----------, *Some Aspects Of Land Reforms In Nepal,* Kathmandu: Regmi Research Project, 1962.

— ------------, *A Study in Nepal Economics History,* 1768-1846, New Delhi: Manjusri Publishing House, 1971.

— -------------, *Thatched Huts and Stucco Palaces*, New Delhi: Vikas Publishing House, 1978.

— Roxborough, Ian, Theories of *Underdevelopment, London*: Mac Millian Co. 1979.

— Rural *Landlessness,* Kathmandu: Intergrated Development System, 1985.

— Sagant, Philip, "Moneylenders and Clan Headman", In C. Malmoud (ed.), *Debt and Debtors*, New Delhi: Vikas Publishing House, 1983.

— Jcott, J.C, *Weapons of the Weak : Everyday Form of Peasant Resistance*, New Heaven: Yale University Press, 1985.

— Seddan, David et al.. *Peasants and Workers In Nepal,* New Delh:, Vikas Publishing House, 1970.

— Shanin, Teodor, Peasant and Peasant Societies, Middlesex: Penguin books, 1975.

— Sharma, Ram *Sharan, Indian Feudalism C 300-1200,* Calcutta: Calcutta University Press, 1962.

— ----------, *Lights On Indian History and Economy,* Calcutta: P.C. Manaktala and sons, 1966.

— *Shrestha BP, "Land Reforms in Nepal", in Nepal: A Profile*, Kathmandu: NCEAR, 1970.

— Singh Suresh, "The Munda Land System of Revenue Reforms in Chhotanagpur During 1869-1908",in R.S. Sharma (ed.) *Land Revenue in India*, New Delhi: Motilal Benarsidass, 1971.

— ----------, The Silent Cry, Kathmandu: Shahayogi Prakashan, 1976.

— Takahasi, Akira, *Land and People In Central Luzon,* Honolulu: University of Hawaii, 1969.

— Ullah, Ata, *Cooperative Movement In Punjab*, London: George Allen and Unwin, 1937.

— Ulyanovski, Rastislav, *Agrarian India Between The World Wars, Moscow*: Progress Publisher, 1985.

— U.N.O., *Land Reforms : Defects In Agrarian Structure*

An Obstacle to Economic Development, New York: United Nations Department of Economic Affairs, 1951.

— Vaidya T.R., *Prithvinarayan Shah: The Founder of Modern Nepal,* New Delhi: Anmol Publication, 1993.

— Vaidya, Tulsi Ram and Manandhar, Tri Ratna, *Crime and punishment* Kathmandu: Bini and Purna, 1985.

— Vansittart, Eden, *Gurkhas: HandBook of The Indian Army*, Calcutta: The Superintendent of Government Printers, 1951.

— Wallinsky, Louis J., *Selected Papers of Wolf Ladejinsky:* Agrarian Reforms As An Unfinished Business, New York: Oxford University Press. 1977.

— Yadav, Shohan Ram, *Nepal Feudalism and Rural Formation*, New Delh: Cosmo Publications, 1984

Books in Hindi :

— Dwivedi, Girija Prasad, Yagnyavlkya Smriti, Lucknow: Nawal Kishore, 1915.

— Shamashatry, R., Kautiliya Arthashastra, Mysore: Raghuveer Printing Press, 1924.

— Srivastav, Kashi Prasad, Nepal Ki Kahani, Delhi: Atma Ram and Sons, 1955.

— Vidyalangkar, P.N., Kautiliya Arthashastra, Lahore: Moti Lal Benarasi Das, 1923.

Books in Nepali :

— Budhathoki, Padam Bahadur, *Nepal Ma Kisan Andolan,* Bhaktapur: the Author, 2048

— Chaguthi, K.B. *Kisan Ko Abastha, Bhaktapur:* Krishna Bhakta Changuthi, n.d.

— Chemjong, BB, *Pallokirat Limbuwanka Magharu*, AsanL: Nepal Press, 2014 B.S.

— Devkota, Grishma Bahadur, *Nepal Ko Rajnaitik Darpan,* Vol. II, Kathmandu: Dhruba B. Devkota, 2036 B.S.

— ------------, *Neplko Rajnaitik Darpan* Vol III, Kathmandu: Upendra B Devkota, 2040 B.S.

— Hhari Lall, *Pahad Mal Bishaya*, Kathmandu: Nepali Bhase Prakasini Samiti, 2008 B.S.

— HMG, *Sixteen Districts and Land Reforms*, (in Nepal), Kathmandu: Department of Land Reforms, 2024 B.S.

— Jyapu, Ram Bahadur, *Nepal Kishan Andolan Ko Ek Jhalak,* Kathmandu: Yuba Sahitya Gosthi, n.d.

— Narahari Nath, Yogi, *Itihas Prakash* Vol 2, Year 2, Kathmandu: Itihas Prakash Mandal, 2012-13 B.S.

— ---------, *Itihas Prakash Ma Sandhi Patra Sangraha,* Dang: Adhyatmik Sammellan, 2022 B.S.

— *Nepali, Chitta Ranjan, Sri 5 Rana Bahadur Shah,* Kathmandu: Ratna Pustak Bhandar, 2044 B.S.

— *Nepal ma Kamaiya Pratha Bhitra Bandha Majdoor,* Kathmandu: INSEC, 2049 B.S.

— Pahadi, Badri Prasad, *Bardiya Jillama Bhumisudhar,* Kathmandu: Department of Land Reforms, 2023 B.S.

— Pasa, Basu, *Pharkera Herda*, Kathmandu: Pasa Publications, 2044 B.S.

— Pokharel, Balakrishna, *Panch Saya Barsha,* Lalitpur: Jagadamba Prakashan, 2031 B.S.

— Sharma, Balchandra, *Nepalko Aitihasik ruprekaha,* Benaras: K.K. Devi, 2022 B.S.

— *Shree 5 Surendra Bikram Shah Ko Pala Ma Baneyko Muluki Ain,* Kathmandu: , Ministry of Law and Justice, 2022 B.S.

— Tuladhar, Bhagwan Ratna, "Nepalko Rajnaitik Vikas Ma Kisan Andolanko Bhumika", *Jhilko* 12, Year 10, No.2, Ashwin 2046 B.S.

Journal Articles In Nepali:

— Lohani, G.P., "Krishi Sambandha ko Aarthik Ra Aitihasik Bhumikabareyko Marx Badi Bisleshan", *Panchayat* p.4, Year 6, No. 9, 2045.

— Singh, Mahan Bikram, "Bhadra 24 Andolan", *Jhilko*, 10:2, 2046.

Journal Articles In English:

— Cox, Thomas, "Land Rights and Ethnic Conflicts In Nepal", *Economic and Political Weekly*, Vol 25, nos. 24-25, June 1990.

— Rothermund, Dietmar, "*Government, Landlords and Tenants In India 1875-1900,* " Reprint from The Indian Economic and History Journal Vol. VI, No. 4, Dec. 1969, Heidelberg, South Asia Institute of the University of Heidelberg, 1969.

— Thapa, Shanker, " An Approach to Peasant Movements in Nepal 1951-60", *Tribhuvan University Journal,* Vol. XIX, June, 1996.

Newspapers

— *Barga Sangharsha* 15, Shrawan 2046.

— *Chalphal* 29 Falgun 2050, 19826 Shrawan 2048.

— *Dristhi* 5 Manghir 2052.

— *Gorkhapatra* Daily, Kathmandu

— *Jhilko* Vol. 17, No. 1 2049, Vol. 12, No. 2, 2046, Vol. 10, No. 2, 2046.

— *Kisan Aawaj* 1:1, Shrawan 2046.

— Kishan Bulletin.

— *Kisan Jagaran* 1:1, 2040.

— *Kopila* Vol. 17, 2038.

— *Mashal* 6:1 Shrawan 2053.

— *Majdoor Kisan.*

— *Mukti Morcha*- 10 Sept. 1979.

— *Nepal Kanon Patrika* 2017, 2018, 2019, 2020 and 2021 issues

— *Nepali Kisan* 1:1, 2044.

— *Panchayat* 64, Year 6, No. 9, 2045.

— *Prakash* 4 Mangsir, 3 Poush 2052

— *Pushpal Smriti Anka.*

— Regmi Research Series different volumes published in the years1974, 1977, 1978, 1979, 1980, 1981, 1982 and 1983 Issues.

— *Tribhuvan University Journal*, Vol. XIX, June 1996.

* * *

GLOSSARY

Abal	:	First grade land with irrigation facility, tow crops are grown in this type of land.
Adhiyan	:	Sharecropping under which half produce of land was divided equally between owners and cultivator at the threasing ground.
Amali	:	Head man of the village. or The functionary responsible for revenue collection and to dispense justice in their areas.
Amanat	:	System of revenue collection.
Ana	:	1/16 of a Rupee.
Andolan	:	Movements for Change
Anebyaj	:	Interest on loans exacted by moneylenders.
Asmani	:	A fine collected while dispensing justice.
Baisi	:	Petty states in the Far Western hill region.
Baksauni	:	A kind of government tax.
Bakyauta Tahasil Adda	:	Government offices in the hills to collect revenue arrear. It preceded the Mal Adda.
Bandhaki	:	Mortgage
Begar	:	Forced and unpaid labour.
Beth	:	Unpaid labour

Bharpai : Receipt issued of tenants at the payment of rent.

Bhedabhada : A tax in Limbu households.

Bhogbandaki : Possessory mortgage.

Bijan : A system of tax assessment in dry land in the hills.

Bigha : Land measurement in the Tarai equivalent to 1.6 Acres.

Birta : Text exempt land grants.

Birta Khareji Adda : Office to manage abolition of Birta land.

Birtawal : The owners of Birta land.

Bisaud : A tax at the rate of 20 %.

Chahar : The lowest grade of land.

Chakchakui : A judicial fine imposed on sexual offences.

Chardam-Theki: A fee paid to confirm rights of cultivation annually.

Chaudhuri : A local revenue collecting functionary in Tarai.

Chhap : A type of Birta land granted for lifetime.

Choke : Interest at the rate of 48 %. on cash loans.

Chumawan : A special levy collected during the sacred thread investiture of princes.

Chuni : Landholders recorded as tax payers in Tarai, or Peasants without Rakam obligation or landholders in the Far Western hill districts.

Damebyaj : A kind of interest in cash.

Dandakunda : A kind of levy.

Darshanbhet : A kind of levy.

Dasaud : Interest at 10 %.

Dhokrey : One who purchased Tirja from the Jagirdars and collected rent.

Dhyake : Interest at the rate of 36 % percent.

Dokebhai : A Limbu who received land from the Limbu Kipatiya.

Dongol : Land measurer in the hill region.
Doyam : A second grade of land to assess tax.
Dristibandhak : Non-possessory mortgage.
Duniya Guthi : Guthi tenure endowed by individuals.
Farse : Relinquishment of title of Birta land by sale.
Gaddimubarak : A levy collected during coronation.
Ghargani : Homestead tax in Tarai.
Ghiukhaney : A levy on rice land in hill.
Gol Rakam : Obligation to supply charcoal.
Guthi : Land endowed for religious and philanthropic purposes.
Guthiyar : Person responsible for the management of Guthi endowments.
Hale : Dry land in the hill region ploughed by an ox team in a day.
Halebij : Dry land to be ploughed for tax assessment under the Bijan system
Halepakho : High quality unirrigated dry land in Bhaktapur district. It yielded a good harvest.
Hali : -Persons who ploughed fields using
ox-teams.
-Bonded labour in Far Western region still in practice.
Hukum : The royal verdict.
Ijaredar : The revenue contractors.
Jagera : The Raikar land not assigned as *Jagir*.
Jagir : Land assigned to the government functionaries in lieu of cash salaries they were entitled to receive.
Jagirdar : One who was beneficiary of the *Jagir* tenure.
Jimidar : Person responsible in collecting land revenue in the Tarai.
Jimidari : The Jurisdiction of a *Jimidar*.
Jimmawals : The local functionaries in the hill region

who could allot land to peasants and collected rent on behalf of the Jagirdars.

Kamaiya : A system of bonded labour in far Western Tarai

Kathet : Land measurer in the Tarai.

Khali-Khandey : Jagir land in which the Kampu Tirja Adda collected rent.

Khet. : Irrigated paddy land in the hill region.

Khuwa : Homestead assigned as Jagir.

Kipat : The communal land tenure.

Kodaley : Dry land in the hill ploughed in one day using a spade.

Kodaleybij : Dry land in the hill region smaller than the Hale holdings. Tax was fixed according to the Bijan system.

Kodaleypakho : Low quality dry land in Bhaktapur yielding less.

Kutey : A small dryland dug by a hoe in a day.

Kut : Rent in land.

Lakhabandhak : Mortgage in which land passes to the second party by the first mortgager.

Lalmohar : The document bearing the royal seal.

Lokabhar : A system under which local people paid stipulated revenue.

Mahasul : Tax levied on certain Birta or Guthi lands.

Magani : A form of tenancy or tenants-at-will.

Mafi : Tax exempt land.

Mal : Land under government proprietorship.

Mal Adda : Revenue office.

Mana : The Smallest Measuring Unit or approximately. - 300 gms of paddy.

Maryo aputali : Escheat property.

Mohi : Tenants/Cultivators.

Mohiboti : Share of tenant cultivators.

Mohinaikey : A local intermediary dealing with the revenue collection in Kathmandu valley

		hill
Muluki Adda	:	The government office performing works of the department of home and judicial affairs.
Muluki Ain	:	The civil code.
Muri	:	-A system of land measurement 4 Muri was equivalent to 1 Ropani. -A unit measuring grains still regulated in Nepal. 20 Pathi consisted of one Muri. It is approximately 50 KG. of paddy.
Pakho	:	Unirrigated dry land.
Pakhureymohi	:	An intermediary tenant.
Parma	:	Exchange of labour.
Pathi	:	A measuring unit for grains, approx.- 2.5 kg of rice.
Patta	:	Certificate of allotted land in the Tarai.
Patuwari	:	Local functionary in Tarai.
Petiya	:	Allowances given to ex-officials, nobility and royalties.
Pota	:	Tax in Birta land in the Kathmandu valley.
		Rahata-byahata
Udanta-Gradanta	:	Arrears, payments and unclaimed property.
Raibandi	:	Periodic redistribution of rice land.
Raikar	:	Land under the proprietorship of the state.
Raiti	:	Land holders or the subjects.
Raja-rajauta	:	The rulers or the kings of the petty feudal states of Baisi and the Chaubisi states.
Raj Guthi	:	The Guthi tenure managed by the Guthi Corporation.
Rajinamah	:	Relinquishment of rights in Raikar through sale.
Rakam	:	Unpaid labour obligation exacted by the state from the peasants cultivating

		Raikar, Kipat and Raj Guthi lands.
Ropani	:	Measurement of land in the hill equivalent to 0.05 hec.
Ryots	:	Tenants
Sdar Dafdar Khana	:	Central Administrative Department.
Salami	:	-A levy paid by the Jagirdars, Talukdars and temple functionaries at appointment or confirmation. -Payments due on the Chhut Guthi. -Tribute paid to landowners.
Sauneyfagu	:	Levy on each roofs in the hill.
Sawaee	:	The rate at one-fourth.
Sayakadi	:	A levy.
Serma	:	Tax on unmeasured dry land.
Sim	:	The third grade of land for.
Sir	:	Land in the Tarai situated between the Churia range and the Majha.
Talsing	:	The landowners
Talukdar	:	Revenue collection functionary in the hill region.
Tamsuk	:	The bonds signed by the debtor
Thekedar	:	The contractor
Tiro	:	Tax or rent.
Tirobandi Andolan	:	A movement against payment of rent (2007-14).
Tiruwa	:	A category of taxable Birta mostly in the Tarai.
Zamindari	:	The landlords in the eastern Tarai and the Baisi region who were very powerful and controlled entire rural people.

* * *

Appendices

Appendix: 1

Chart No. 1
The structure of Nepalese society during the Rana regime.

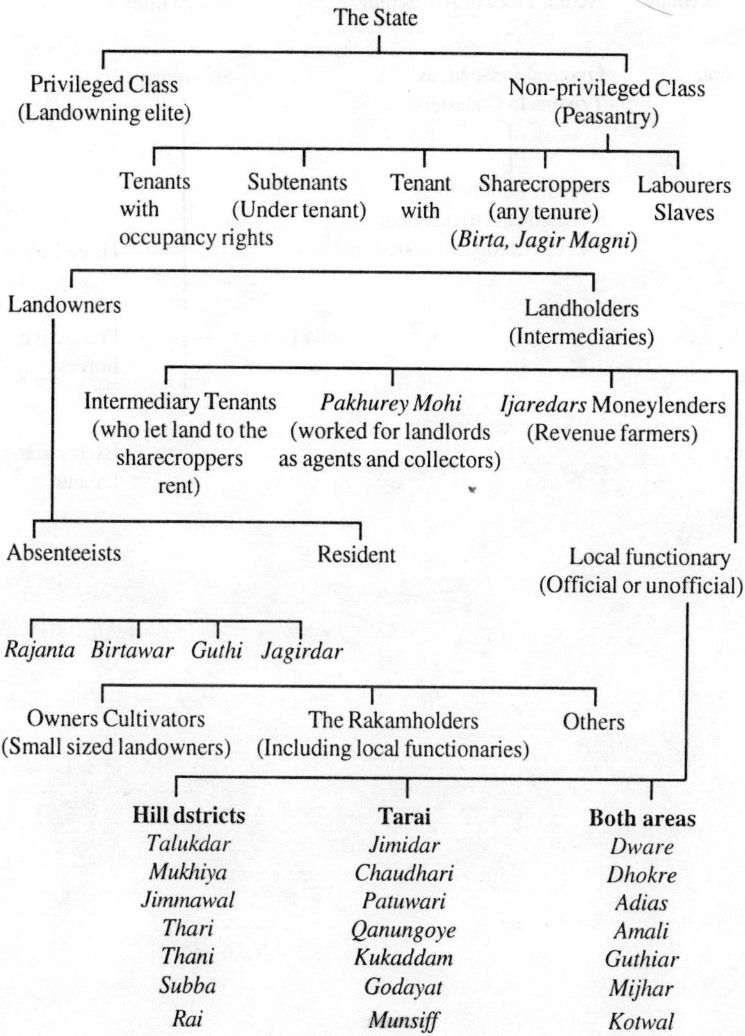

Appendix: 2

Chart No.2
The Format Of Production Relation In Raikar

1. Raikar Land:

Tax Sharer — State

Actual Tiller or shares rent — Ownership Regd, as Tenants In Cadasters → Become Landholders if rented land to peasants for cultivation and shared rent

Actual tiller — Sub-tenants

- Hired Labour
- Family Labour — Productive Forces
- Exchanged Labour

Appendix: 3

Chart No: 3
Production Relations in Raikar Derivatives:

2. The Raikar Derivatives : Birta, Guthi, and Jagir Tenures

- **State** — The ultimate proprietor although it granted immediate land rights to individuals absentee land lords
- **Landowners** — The beneficiaries were the Raja-Rajautas, Birta owners, Hired Jagirdars, and the Guthi institutions. They were the absentees who rented land for cultivation and exacted rent
- **Intermediary** — The landholders or the rent receiving intermediaries who took care of land and worked on behalf of the
- **Tenants Cultivators**
  - Family Labour
  - Productive
  - Hired Labourers
  - Exchanged Labour

* Thus, the production relation in Nepal in the 19th and 20th Centuries was as follows-

- The Absentees or big landlords
- Intermediary
- Tenants
- Sub Tenants

- Production Relations
  - Owners Cultivators
  - Wage Labourers
    - Family Labour
    - Hired Labour

Appendix: 4

Chart No. 4
Contemporary Production relations: in Raikar and Guti tenures:

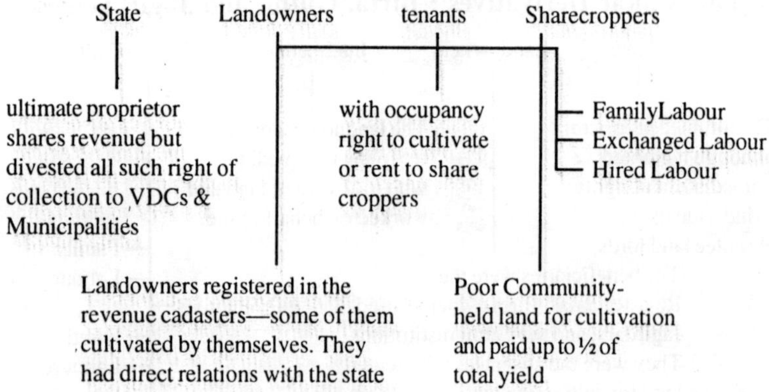

Appendix: 5

Chart No. 5
Changes in the old structure

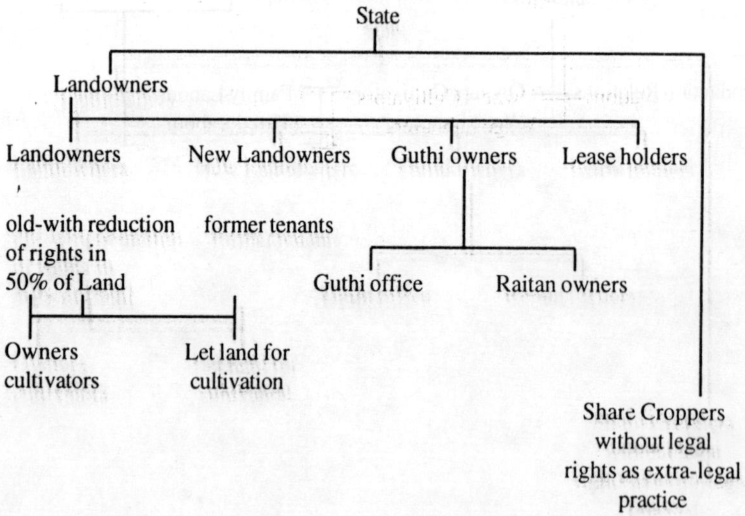

Appendix: 6

List of Traditional levies:

Customary levies collected during Nineteenth and Twentieth Centuries in Nepal.

Abuwab	Fattehmubarak	Nwagi Kharchha
Asmani	Furryat	Pota
Balbithauri	Futkar	Puchhai
Bankar	Gaddhimubarak	Purohityain
Baragandi	Ghar Khharcha	Rajanka (Godan, Chumawan and Goddimubarak)
Beth-begar	Ghargadni	Sagaudha
Bhadabhar	Ghiukhaney	Sahanpal
Bhedabhada	Ghiukhaney	Sair
Bhota-Pota	Ghoddhuwa	Salami
Bhubahal	Godan	Saliana
Bhusawan	Goddhuwa	Samriti
Bighahatti	Gunahagari	Sanyashi Mandali
Bihadani	Guran	Sarba Chandrayan
Chandachira	Hasil	Sauney Fagu
Chanurahi	Hattidana	Sera
Charai	Jalkar	Serma
Chardam theki	Jhara	Singarahat
Charirakam	Jogi Mandali	Sirto
Charsa	Kajkalayan Ko Walak	Sundhuwai
Chhalahi	Kathiyari	Tal
Chhito Chhap	Khar Chari	Tika
Chiyai	Khur Chhapi	Tikabhet
Chumawan	Khurpa Thek	Tile Dhupey
Danda	Kusai Bisai	Tip
Dhalwa Pathi	Lama Pathi	Toana
Dhanda-Kunda	Mahasul	Walak
Dharmadhikar	Mahasul Mandali	
Dip	Mejmani	
Doko Boko	Mudhai	
Doley	Nirkhi	
Dungakar	Moto	

Index

A

Abolition of Birta Tenure 103
Abolition of Traditional Land Tenures 109
Absentee Landlords 26, 27, 38, 39, 79
___ Individual 120
Acharya, Babu Ram 90
Activities of Peasant Class 134
Activities of Peasants Community 124
Activities of Peasants in Butawal 116
Actual Cultivators 25, 49
Agents of State 135
Agrarian
___ Activities and Peasants Discontent 127
___ Conditions in Terai and Hills 140
___ Economy in the *Rana Period* 39—*Fenda Set-up*
___ History of Nepal 110
___ From 1846 to 1951 117
___ Landmarks in the 164
___ Relations in Nepal Under Ranas 166
___ Social Structure 32
— in the country 65
—of the country–existing 29
—Hierarchical 32
___ Structure in Rana 28, 53
___ in Nepal 32
___ System 64, 134
___ System of a Nation 14
___ Nepal 18, 160, 162
Agricultural Production Activities 61
Agricultural Situation in Nepal 131
Akhil Nepal Kisan Sangh 139,169
Alternative Source of Income 132
Analysis of Agrarian Production Relations 68
Anti-Rana Movement 9
Asian Countries 124
Asian Indigenous System 33
Asian System of State Landlordism 36
Aspects of Nepal's Land Holding System 8
Aspects of Nepalese Agriculture 172

B

Backward System of Agriculture and Landholding, 124
Bardia Commission 143, 145

"Bardia Land Commission", 30
Basic Nature of Agrarian Society 20.
Basic Trends in Agrarian Relations in South Asia 62
Big Landlords 3, 26
Birta
___ Abolition Act, 164
___ cultivators and Tenants 154
___ owners 154
___ owners and Jagirdars 132, 136
___ owners and other Landlords 104
___ owners, Right of 132
___ System 101
___ Taxation Act of 1906 128
___ Tenants 102
Brahmin Moneylenders 113
British India 25, 49
British Rulers in India 3
Budhathdki, Padma Bahadur 169, 170
Burden of Customary Levies 117
Butawal
___ Area 140, 141
___ Land Commission of 1951 1, 42

C

Changes in Land ownerships in Bardia 144
Chuni Ryots, 98
Civil Code of 1854 37, 90
Chuni Ryots Common Problems of Traditional Agrarian Society 19
Conceptualized Terminology of Middle Peasants 56
Condition of Peasantry 4, 138
___ in Nepal 134
Conditions of Nepalese Cultivators 50
Conditions of Nepalese Peasants and Cultivators 32
Contemporary Agrarian Society 45
Contemporary Nepalese Society 16
Core Aspect of the Agrarian Relationship 60
Consequences for Peasant Economy 133
Cultivating Community 121
___ Tenants 79
Cultivators of the coutnry 1
Cultivators of Nepal 64
Cultivators in all Tenures 70

D

Dang Valley 114
Democratic Leaders 114

E

Eastern Nepal 113
Economic Activities of a Traditional Society 1
Economy of Nepal 47
End of English Doctrine of Rent 160
End of Rana Rule 42, 156
Essential Part of Nepal's Agrarian System 41
Establishment of Various Peasant's Organisations 168
Evolution of Land Laws 67
Evolution of Private Property Right on Raikar 99
Existing Landholding System in Nepal 138

Exploitation of the Peasant 114

F

Feudal Aspect of Land Ownership 174
Feudal Nature of Nepalese Society 146
Financial Condition of Peasant Community 8
Food & Agricultural Organisation 20
Force of Production for Centuries 12
Formation of Peasant Forces 12

G

Gaunda Dailekh 72
Goal of Professional Peasant Organisation 151
Government of Nepal 137
Grand Survey of 1925 84
Group of Intermediaries 42
Guth Land 166
Guthi Institutions 167

H

Hamilton, Francis Buchanan 47
Heterogeneous Society of Nepal 2
Higher Strata in Agrarian Hierarchy 5
History of Agriculture 1
History of Middle and Working Class Agitation 124
History of the Rana Autocracy 45
Hobsbawm—observation of 57

I

Ijaredars 93, 103, 162
Impact of Communist Ideology 175
Importance Aspect in Agricultural Growth 4
Importance of Terai 3
Important
___ Aspects of Agricultural Development 3
___ Feature of the Contemporary Agrarian System 33
___ Movements Led by Nepali Congress 115
Indigenous Traditional System 160
Individual Landowners 120
Institutionalization of Peasant Society 174

J

Jagera Land 70, 92
___ cultivators of 77
Jagir and Birta 166
Jagir—*Khangi* Land 73
Jagir Land in Terai 108
Jagirdar 92
Jagirdars and Birtawalas 7
___ and Tenants 106
Jetha—raiyat 43
Jamidari System 18, 44, 135

K

Kamaiya System 52, 142, 147
___ Impact of 136
Karnali Region 46
___ and Tarai 97, 98
Kathmandu Valley 43, 103, 105, 108, 115, 136, 150, 151, 167, 170
___ Peasants in the 162, 173
Kautilya's Arthashastra 41, 68, 95
Khangi Land of Various Jagirdars 77

Khet and *Pakho* Land 129
Kinua Bita 92
Kirkpatrick 39-40
Kut Movement in Kathmandu 115
Kut System
___ in the Hill Region 18
___ Introduction of the 39
___ in the Twentieth Century 41

L

Land
___ Acquisition Act 100
___ Act of 1957, 24, 47, 103, 108, 110, 112, 153, 172.
___ Act of 1964 49, 51, 52, 74
___ Commission in Terai 139
___ holding Intermediaries 69
___ and Local Revenue Functionaries 76
___ holding Practices 165
___ holding rights in Raiker 96
___ holding and Tenurial Condition in Nepal 131
___ Practices 165
___ lords of Nepal 49
___ lords—Tenants Relations 145
___ lords and Tenants—Significant factors 82
___ lords in Villages 38
___ mark in Agrarian History of Nepal 53
___ mark in the Evolution of Cultivators' Right son Raikar Land 38
___ mark in the History of Evolution of Peasants Land Rights 96
___ owners in Bardia 143
___ owners in Landholding Intermediaries 37
___ ownership in Nepal 3
___ owning Community 69
___ Land Reform Act 112, 157, 172
___ Amendment 158
___ of 1964 88, 91, 95, 108, 113, 138, 152, 163, 164
___ Commission 151, 153, 169
___ Revenue Act 87
___ System in Nepal—Characteristics of the 32
___ Tenure System in Nepal 89
Landed Aristocracy and Birta owning Ranas 146
Landon Perceval 19
Ledijinsky, Wolf 50
Leftist Movement 168
Lenin 55, 62
___ Mao Tse Tung 56
Lenin's Division of Peasants 14
Local Talukdars 35

M

Magni System 90
Main Categories of Intermediaries 43-44
Main Duties of a Jimmawal 80
Major Form of Property 2
Major Forms of Tenure 165
Manusmriti 15, 68
Mary, Karl 25
___ and Fredrick Engels 54
Marxian view 54, 55
Marxist Ideology 115
Marxist Literature 5
___ outlook on Peasant 55
Medieval Feudal and Autocratic Rulers 145
Medieval Feudalism 117
Movements agains Landlords 115

Mughal Empire, 16
Mughal Rule in India 44, 48
Muluki Ain (N) 1854 105

N

Nature of Landowning Elite Activities 171
Nepal's
___ Agricultural System 19
—Important Characteristics of the 19
___ Agrarian Relations—Important Factors in 85
___ Landholding System 47
—Significant Aspect of 8
Nepali Congress 10, 137, 147, 152, 170
___ Nepali Communist Party 113, 117
Nepalese
___ Agrarian System 14
___ Communists 126
___ Gentry 2, 139
___ Landowning Elites 66
___ Peasantry 9, 13, 48, 53, 124, 127, 135, 152
—Conditions of the 50
—Legacy of Ruthless Exploitation of the 11
___ Society and its Economy 160
Network of Traditional Relationship 66
Newari Folk Song 160

O

Old System of Rent Assessment 170
Owners of *Birta* and *Jagir* Tenures 67

P

Pant, Bhumi Dutt 116
Panchayat Regime 174
Paradigm of Agrarian Structure 20
Paradigm of Leftwing Parties 13
Parasitic Community 54
Pattern of Agrarian and Production Relations in Nepal 65
Pattern of Land Central 32
Pattern of Landholding 30
Peasant Community 36, 58, 89, 117, 123, 147
___ Leaders 151
___ Movement 10, 115, 116, 139, 171
—Series of 164
Peasants in Nepal 163
___ in Rural Kathmandu 170
People in Agrarian Society 27
Policies of the Ranas 40
Political Economists of Nepal 33
Practical Aspect of Nepalese Agriculture 13
Pre-Rana-Shah Rule 21
Primary Aim of Rana Administration 43
Principle Force in Production Process 135
Privileged and non-privileged classes 149
Process of
—de Peasantization 56
—monetization 161
—Transfer of Land Rights 2
Promulgation of Land Act 29

R

Raiker
___ Land 73, 94, 97

___ Registered Tenant in the 91, 112
___ Tenants 34, 72, 93, 96
—in the Terai Regions 97
___ Tenure 97
Rana Period in Nepal 49
Rana Regime 2, 3, 5, 6, 7, 12, 21, 29, 32, 57, 67, 74, 81, 83, 86, 117, 118, 152, 163, 171, 172
___ Agrarian Relations During the 88
___ Assessment During the 128
___ Emergence of 124
___ End of 63, 100, 122, 125, 149, 155
Rana Rule 152, 162
Rana Rulers 135, 148
Rates of Sauneyfagu Levy 118
Regmi, Mahesh Chandra 48, 51
Reformists Politicians 137
Relationship between Landlords and Tenants 75
Remnants of Medieval Feudalism 59
Rent Control and Tenancy Security 112
Resident Cultivators 90
Rich Landlords in villages 148
Right of Rent Collection 6
Role of Peasantry until 1951 36
Rulers of Nepal 139
Ruling Elite 132, 135

S

Scot, J.C. 138
Second Half of Nineteenth Century 160
Seven Tenures 29
Shah, Prithvi Narain 47
Shah Regime 29
Share croppers 81, 121, 151
Social Groups in Nepal 28
Sociology of Nepalese Agriculture 126
State's Landlordism 46
Structural Hierarchy of Agrarian Communities 33
Structural Pattern of an Agrarian Society 15
Structure of Agrarian Society 62
___ Nepalese 22
Superstructure of Agrarian Relations 11
System of Agriculture and Agrarian Relations 114
System of Ryotwari in Bombay 46

T

Talukdars 72, 80, 85, 86, 99
Tenancy Right Acquisition Act 82, 86, 139, 155
Tenant Cultivators 141
Tenants of all kinds 77
Tenants in Nepal 82
Tenants of *Rakam* Land 73
Tennurial Conditions and Status of Cultivators in Tenures 132
Terai Districts 11
Territory of Kumaon 125
Tharu Settlement in the Terai 114
Tirobandi Andolan 167
Traditional Agrarian Relations 59
—in Nepal 69
—Types of 86
Traditional Agrarian System 163
Traditional Land Tenure in Nepal 18
Traditional Type of *Ain Sawal* 156
Traditional Type of Inter-relationship 122

Transfer of Landownership Rights 135
Transfer of Tenancy Rights 164

U

Ultimate Properitor of Land Property 35
Ulyanovsky, Rostislav 48
Unequal Pattern of Landownership 65
Unequal Pattern of Relationship 67

V

Village Landlords and Moneylenders 49
Village Panchayat 164

W

Wages of Agrarian Labourers in 1951 137
Western Terai 140
___ Conditions of Peasantry 147
___ and Eastern Terai 135
Worst Forms of Tenancy 146

Y

Yajnavalkya 42

Z

Zamindars 78, 155, 140, 141, 145, 146
___ Primary and Intermediary 44
___ in the Terai and Karanali Regions 95
___ Usurius 74
___ and Patwaris 142, 144
Zamindari in Bengal 63
Zamindari Seers 146, 147